Lessons and Laughs from the
International "Best Boss/Worst Boss" Contests

BEST BOSS

WORST BOSS

JAMES B. MILLER

A Fireside Book
Published by Simon & Schuster

FIRESIDE
Rockefeller Center
1230 Avenue of the Americas
New York, NY 10020

Copyright © 1996 by Jim Miller

All rights reserved,
including the right of reproduction
in whole or in part in any form.

First Fireside Edition 1998
Published by arrangement with The Summit Publishing Group

FIRESIDE and colophon are registered trademarks of Simon & Schuster Inc.

Manufactured in the United States of America

1   3   5   7   9   10   8   6   4   2

Library of Congress Cataloging-in-Publication Data
Miller, James B. (James Bernard)
Best boss worst boss: lessons and laughs from the international
"best boss/worst boss" contests/James B. Miller
p.   cm.
Originally published: Arlington, Texas: The Summit Publishing Group, 1996
1. Executives–Professional ethics–Case studies.   2. Management–Moral and ethical
aspects–Case studies.   3. Corporations–Corrupt.
HD38.2.M553   1998
658.4'09'0207–dc21   98-18606
CIP

ISBN 0-684-84639-X

To my wife Joan

For all her help and support, not only in assisting with the publication of this book and my first book, The Corporate Coach, *but also for the encouragement she has given me during our marriage. Her positive influence has been a major reason for the successes that I have enjoyed, not only in business, but also in life. Because of her, I have to be the luckiest man alive!*

∾

CONTENTS

ACKNOWLEDGMENTS

FOR THE ENCOURAGEMENT and support of this book, I will always be grateful to my wife Joan, our sons Michael and Greg, and daughter Kathy for their continued love, patience, and acceptance of my management style.

Sharon Wells, my assistant. Without her efforts there would be no *Best Boss, Worst Boss* book. A special thanks to her for all that she did not only in writing this book, but also for screening thousands of the essays we received to determine which ones would be the most beneficial to the readers. For coordinating the past "Best Boss/Worst Boss" contests and for her assistance in helping to set up a marketing program to help promote the book.

Kay Smith, my secretary. For all her help and assistance during the past fifteen years, including her patience in the screening of essays for *Best Boss, Worst Boss* and also for her suggestions and criticism as they relate to this book.

All the employees worldwide, who have entered our "Best Boss/Worst Boss" contests in the past. You have helped provide much of the material that was used in this book.

Len Oszustowitcz, publisher and CEO of The Summit Publishing Group. Every author should be as fortunate as I am to be able to work with Len. A special thanks to him for all of his assistance in writing *Best Boss, Worst Boss* and for his enthusiasm for the book itself. The total commitment that he has for the success of this book has been an inspiration to me.

Bill Scott and Mark Murphy, my editors at The Summit Publishing Group, for their input and patience on this book.

Sandy Madison, whose illustrations help set the mood, and also David Sims, who designed the cover.

The employees at BT Office Products International, Inc., Business Interiors, and American Discount Office Furniture.

The media, nationwide, for their past support of the annual "Best Boss/Worst Boss" contest. Without their cooperation, we would not have been able to enjoy the success we did as it relates to the number of entries that we received each year during the contest.

A special thanks to Larry McShane of the Associated Press and to Christopher Ave of the *Arlington Morning News*, for the special coverage they have provided over the years to make employees aware of the contest.

I LOVE TO LAUGH. And the incredible antics of some of the characters in Jim Miller's *Best Boss, Worst Boss*–the result of his popular, annual international "Best Boss/Worst Boss" contest– had me howling.

But there is much more here than a recounting of the foibles of some really, extraordinarily bad bosses. Jim has woven together valuable and important lessons for us as bosses *and* employees. In the tradition of his best-selling *The Corporate Coach*, Jim analyzes the conduct of these bosses, points out the probable explanations for their behavior and–most importantly–tells us how to deal with the bad ones and emulate the good.

At a time when good leadership is more important to the business world than ever, it is sad to learn of the seven-to-one ratio of bad bosses to good bosses who were entered in the "Best Boss/Worst Boss" contest. Like Jim, I don't believe that this reflects the actual ratio of good to bad bosses in this country, but it is clear that there are too many bad bosses. We just can't afford them anymore. If you're one, perhaps you'll see a reflection of yourself inside these pages and will be inspired to make a change for the better. At any rate, it's a sure bet that your employees will recognize you and at least they'll have some clues as to how to maintain morale and productivity in spite of the anchor that's weighing them down–you!

Congratulations to all the good bosses. You're more than just good managers, you are true leaders. You undoubtedly have more friends than employees, and I have no doubt that your company prospers as a result of your efforts and that of those who work for you.

Whether you're a boss or have a boss, there are interesting and important business lessons here that you won't get from any university.

My thanks to Jim Miller for once again showing us that the route to business success is happy employees and happy customers—and for doing so in a most delightful and entertaining manner.

Ron Zemke
Author of *Service America* and
Knock Your Socks Off Service® series

INTRODUCTION

IN MANY BOOKS, the introduction is used to give the reader a running start into the book. This book is different. In *Best Boss, Worst Boss,* I want to use the introduction to answer two questions. The first is why I wrote the book and the second is how the book should be read.

After reading the responses to our many years of "Best Boss/Worst Boss" Contests, I had my eyes opened to an amazing spectrum of working conditions across the country. We learned of great bosses whose generosity, kindness, and honesty warmed our hearts and reaffirmed our belief in human dignity and goodness. On the other hand, we saw a shocking level of employee mistreatment that deeply bothered us.

Therefore, this book was written to give a wake-up call to business leaders to remember that without good, happy employees, their ability to compete effectively in the long term is doubtful.

I talk a lot in this book about the long term. That's because we live in the long term. Most folks are good and they're trying their level best to provide their families a good life. They are willing to work long and hard in exchange for a little slice of comfort in their old age. These goals don't call for short-term fixes. Most people work almost fifty years during their lifetimes. They realize that life is a long haul and that short-term fixes don't pay the bills or provide for the education of their kids or for their retirement.

The same applies to bosses and to the companies they represent. Short-term thinking doesn't build clients for life, doesn't build market share, and generally doesn't succeed.

Bosses and their employees are tied together in their mutual quest for long-term success. They've got to learn to live and prosper together for years on end. My main goal in writing this book has been to reemphasize what it takes for employees and their bosses to work together over the long term. It takes honesty. It takes trust. It takes fairness. It takes respect.

Each chapter of this book looks at a quality that must be present in a healthy employee-boss relationship. It offers examples of great bosses who exhibit that quality and, unfortunately, many more who don't.

The examples are taken from the thousands of entries to our annual contests that we've received over the past years. We found ourselves continually amazed at the sheer magnitude of the response we received. Employees from every part of the workforce wrote to share experiences about their bosses...good and bad. We marveled at the similar characteristics—like trust, respect, fair treatment, and empowerment—that the good bosses shared. We shook our heads in disbelief as we read about bad bosses who cheated, lied, spied, controlled, and manipulated their employees.

Some entries were too long, too late, or dealt with litigation that ruled them ineligible as a winner, but still people wrote, and wrote, and continue to write. Some employees even called our offices to elaborate on their experiences. It truly has been amazing to see the outpouring of emotions that the contest generated. Unfortunately, it is a sad fact that the responses we received run about seven to one, bad boss to good boss. I really don't believe that the ratio of bad to good bosses is that lopsided. Instead, I think that it's just human nature to spend more time complaining than praising. People with bad bosses are a lot more likely to enter the contest than are people with good bosses.

We hope that as you read the letters you will see yourself, and evaluate your behavior. Most of us can see ourselves in some of the letters, and I think that it's important to reflect honestly on what we see. If improvement is necessary I hope that we'll make the adjustment.

At this point I'd also like to note that we're *ALL* bosses. Every boss has his or her boss! And we boss not just those at work—how about families? Our communities? Our churches? Everyone who touches another's life is a part of a relationship that is essentially the same as the employee-boss relationship. The same rules and challenges apply.

The bottom line, then, is that I wrote this book to help us all learn how to get along better—specifically at work, but if those lessons carry over to home and beyond, so much the better!

Now, a few thoughts on how to read this book. As I said above, I have divided it into characterizations of good and bad bosses. Each chapter is built around the letters we actually received, and these letters generally make several points, not just the ones we're discussing in that particular chapter. Therefore, even though a letter is included in a given section, it may talk about other matters as well–so you get a bonus! It's best to read each letter; pull the main point from it, and then use the rest of the information as background to get a better feel for the people involved.

Now, speaking of people, they come in two kinds, male and female. So do bosses. Unfortunately, trying to include both genders gets pretty awkward, and so I have just used masculine gender in discussions that apply equally to male and female bosses or employees. I hope that this does not offend anyone; no one is meant to be excluded. However, I think it might have been even more offensive to fill the book with alternative pronouns, leaving each reader to wade through the confusion himself/herself!

I have also provided comments among the letters, each one based upon decades of my experience and the management of thousands of employees. I hope that these will help the reader to *think* about what the letters are saying. There are valuable lessons in these letters, and each is worth serious consideration. I hope that my comments will help you do that.

As you may know already, I am also the author of a previous book about business, *The Corporate Coach*. In that book, I look at business in detail and provide insight on every phase of it. I do the same to the employee-boss relationship here by summarizing the key points covered in each chapter in a section called "The Corporate Coach's Comments." In this section I provide specific suggestions on how to deal with touchy issues that arise every day in the relationship between employees and their bosses. I can't guarantee that they'll work in every situation. However, based on my experience, they should provide a good starting place. I hope you'll find them useful and I hope you'll use these as quick references long after you've finished reading the book.

Finally, I want to congratulate you on reading this book. By doing so, you prove your concern for making the employee-boss relationship a positive one. I think you'll agree that the stories, comments, and lessons in this book all reinforce one fundamental principle: We all want to be treated with respect and dignity– no matter who's the boss.

CHAPTER 1

Scrooges and Santas

STINGINESS AND GENEROSITY mean different things to different people. Countless marriages, families, and friendships have been destroyed because of the differences in how people deal with money. So why should we expect that it would be any different in business? On the job, where people work shoulder to shoulder, day in and day out, money can drive a wedge between even the most cooperative of folks.

Nowhere in business is the "I have it and I want more of it" problem of stinginess more obvious than in the relationship between employee and boss. The very reason most people go to work is to earn money and get ahead, so there's bound to be a problem when a boss is perceived to be a cheapskate! But the key word here is "perceived."

Our letters are full of examples of a bad boss being characterized as having a "Scrooge-like" nature because he is too tight. But beware! What seems "cheap" to one person might be "thrifty" to another. But we'll save that discussion for a little later. First, let's look at a few examples from letters we received where there can be no doubt...these bosses are CHEAP, CHEAP, CHEAP!

MY BOSS makes Scrooge seem like Santa Claus! She saves money by turning the thermostat off...we wear coats and gloves in winter and wilt in sleeveless tops in the one-hundred-degree summer heat. She saves on the electricity bill by not allowing us to use electric lights. The only light available is the sunlight that enters through the windows. Even worse, the one employee toilet has to be flushed by pouring a bucket of water into the toilet bowl.

∽

TO CUT COSTS AND CONSERVE WATER, my boss will not flush the toilet. He never chips in when the office staff orders food, but he's always right there with outstretched hands when it arrives. He travels often and has his secretary write letters of disapproval to motels that he frequents so he can get a free room there the next time around. At business lunches, he always makes a scene and complains about his food so the restaurant will reduce or "comp" his meal. He constantly borrows employees' vehicles so he doesn't have to put mileage on his company-supplied lease car. If he likes an employee's picture hanging on the wall, he thinks nothing about taking it for his own office, without saying a word.

∽

WITH THE PERSONALITY OF A DIAL TONE, our cheap-skate boss even separates two-ply toilet tissue in order to make two rolls for the employee bathroom. He refuses to give us our annual reviews on time. So we don't get a raise for the entire year. When the office receives award points that are redeemable for free gifts to be distributed to employees, the boss keeps them all for himself.

∽

WE CALL HER THE WARDEN, and she's the cheapest, most paranoid human being I've ever met. She locks up the coffee, hand soap, paper towels, and toilet paper in the vault because she believes that we steal from her. She even counts the cardboard inserts in the toilet paper to make sure none is missing. Our wages have been frozen for three years, along with the pension and profit sharing plan, and she has fought management tooth and toenail to not give us raises.

∽

HE'S THE STINGIEST, greediest boss in the world! It seems he really couldn't justify a raise this year even though our production was increased by 92 percent. My Christmas bonus consisted of moldy old food and canned goods with six-month-old expiration dates despite the fact that this monster's net income increased by $100,000 last year!

∼

IT'S CHRISTMAS EVE. Picturesque snow drifts into the darkening afternoon and Scrooge, the dentist, promised we could leave at noon. A patient arrived with a toothache and Doc discovers the patient has insurance and convinces him that he needs a five-hundred-dollar gold crown...a procedure which keeps me in the office until well after five o'clock. I'm not paid overtime nor for sick leave. I supposedly get a Christmas bonus, but have never seen a cent. Once he ordered uniforms, at my expense, and didn't like them when they arrived. You guessed it...I had to buy others! With his $200,000-a-year practice, he reminds me when it's "my turn" to buy coffee!

These excerpts are clear examples of those we received that portray bosses who have an unrealistic perspective of the value of a dollar versus the value of a person. Having been the boss to thousands during my years in business, I have learned the immeasurable value of good employees. Unfortunately, many bosses take a short-term view of "success" and try to wring the last dollar out of each buck *today*, totally forgetting that the real test of success is how the company performs over the long term. And the evidence is clear—to be a long-term success, bosses must have long-term, happy employees. Trust me; treating employees generously may seem like an expense, but it is an investment that yields a huge return over the long haul.

Inexpensive Generosity

The amazing thing about generosity is that it doesn't have to be expensive! As I said previously, generosity is often just a matter of perception. Most employees are realistic. They realize that it is expensive to run a business. And besides, they realize that if the business isn't making money, there will be no jobs for anyone—including the boss.

My experience has been that it's often the little things that make an employee think that the boss is cheap. Look at the excerpts we reprinted above. They talk about heating and cooling the office, not flushing the toilet to save water, trying to get free meals, stealing pictures, award points, coffee, and even (for goodness' sake) toilet tissue. A vast majority of the complaints about bad bosses are based on little, inexpensive things, not thousands of dollars.

The point we must remember is that most cheap bosses could turn around their image, not to mention their employees' morale, with little things. A free lunch on occasion, a couple of hours off with pay as a surprise, a fruit basket at Christmas, a birthday card, free sodas, or maybe just a nice, clean work space. These are not going to make much difference in the profitability of 99.9 percent of companies. And even if it is a small but significant expense, how expensive is it compared to the cost of recruiting, interviewing, hiring, training, and motivating a new employee? I guarantee you that you can buy a lot of toilet paper for the cost of replacing just one employee who decides he or she couldn't live one more day with a boss who is CHEAP!

Just for fun, let's play with some figures. How much toilet paper can you buy with what you have to spend to replace an employee who quits because the boss is too cheap?

How Much Toilet Paper Can You Buy For the Cost of Replacing One Employee?

Newspaper advertisement for a replacement	$100
Time from staff to interview (ten one-hour interviews, interviewer earns $40,000 per year)	$200
Reference checks, etc.	$100
Meetings on candidate	$100
Telephone calls, faxes, etc.	$100
Orientation, indoctrination, and introduction	$300

Training	$1,000
Getting up to speed (new hire takes six weeks to contribute at $30,000 per year)	$3,461
Mistakes, missed opportunities, etc.	????
Aggravation during training, etc.	????
Toll on employee morale, etc.	????
Total Cost (at very least)	**$5,361**
Cost per roll of toilet paper	.35
Number of rolls you could have bought with what it cost to hire a new $30,000 employee	**15,317**

I'm being ridiculous, you say. Am I really? Maybe if cheapskate bosses went through an exercise like this, they would finally figure out what is meant by the phrase "penny-wise and pound-foolish." But don't forget the main point. I'm not saying don't be cheap with employees because it's nicer if you are generous. (Of course it is!) The message here is that bosses can often actually make *more* money by being a little more generous!

Recognition is Free!

Another way for bosses to beat the cheapskate blues is to consider for a moment the value of recognition. Many companies reward their people for superior performance and attitude with some sort of recognition. While money is soon spent and trips fade away in photo albums, the recognition spotlight warms employees for a long time. Ribbons, engraved plaques, and trophies are an extremely inexpensive way to convey to employees that they are valuable to your company, and it has been proven over and over that simple recognition can take the place of many dollars when it comes to making employees feel important. Try using "YOU ARE TERRIFIC" certificates to convey how much your employees mean to you. Send letters of praise to the employees' homes so their families can see how important the employees are to you and how much you appreciate them. Publish their pictures and articles about their successes in company newsletters. Post in the work area complimentary letters from customers about employees for everyone to see. Even cookies and candy can go a long way if they're wrapped in appreciation.

I remember a forty-nine-cent plastic tiger that was presented to the top salesperson each month at a company where I worked early in my career. FORTY-NINE CENTS! And the sales force worked like crazy to win that "Tiger of the Month" award and to display that treasure proudly on their desks. It isn't only about money. It's about appreciation. It is possible to motivate, reward, and even be considered generous without breaking the bank.

Below are excerpts from letters about some good bosses with the right idea. Let's see what makes them so special.

EACH CHRISTMAS our boss dresses up as Santa and goes around to each of our locations to give the employees a candy cane or rock candy. Once when an employee's father was dying in an out-of-state hospital, our boss generously gave the employee a week of his own vacation and paid for his flight so the employee could be at his father's side. He even gave me a frequent flier round-trip ticket for two for anywhere in the US in appreciation for my hard work.

~

ONE BIRTHDAY, Dale surprised me with a gigantic card containing five hundred dollars, and he sent me and my husband on a trip, paying for our airline tickets and hotel. One summer day, he announced that he had arranged for someone to answer the phone, and he was taking us to the movies! He even bought the popcorn!

~

EVEN THOUGH HE WAS THE PRESIDENT of Lockheed at the time, Gordon would don a Santa hat each Christmas and lead a parade of trams through the mile-long factory, handing out trinkets and memorabilia, and individually wishing everyone a happy holiday season.

~

GINNY WAS A POLICEWOMAN, but her love for kids led her into education where I met and worked for her as a vice principal for seventeen years. She was generous with her time, praise, encouragement, love, and laughter. I've watched her leave school to take underprivileged students to purchase a warm jacket or clothing at her own expense, because they were too embarrassed to come to school. Many times she took a student to the market to buy groceries because there was no food at home.

～

PETER IS A RHODES SCHOLAR AND A LAWYER, who has successfully balanced his priorities while displaying enormous generosity to his employees. For Secretary's Day he presented me with a free, round-trip airline ticket anywhere in the US, as well as a generous bonus at Thanksgiving "in thanksgiving for all I do for him." After overhearing that my lifelong wish was to see Barbra Streisand, my boss and his wife purchased a Gold Circle ticket to her concert and it truly was my dream come true!

～

SPENCER REWARDS THE WHOLE OFFICE by frequently inviting us to breakfast, lunch, and dinner. His generosity includes expense-paid vacations to Lake Tahoe, Utah, Hawaii, Las Vegas, Puerto Vallarta, Florida, Key West, Cancun, Cozumel, Bahamas, and recently our third cruise to the Caribbean. He has told me that if money is ever the issue for my seeking another job, he will outbid any other employer.

～

RONALD IS ONE OF THE MOST COMPASSIONATE and generous family practitioners ever...not just to his patients, but especially to his employees. When the brakes went out on my car, he handed me his credit card and told me to get them fixed. When the Omaha Ballet brought Baryshnikov to town, the only way you could get tickets was to purchase season tickets to the ballet. He gave me his tickets so that my daughter and I could enjoy six wonderful ballets. He springs regularly for treats like ice cream for the office staff, and because he is a gourmet chef, he often prepares breakfast or lunch for us.

These are good examples of bosses who understand that generosity comes in many flavors. Some of the examples are of nice, but very inexpensive things that obviously made a big impression on an employee. Rock candy, a trip to the movies, or a warm jacket are examples of little things that mean a lot. The larger acts of generosity, such as frequent flier miles or a week of vacation, are wonderful and obviously represent great acts of personal kindness. I commend those with the resources and desire to sustain such generosity. But just because there are not millions of dollars in the till, don't assume that it's time to put on the Scrooge act.

Cheapness May be in the Eye of the Beholder

In fairness, no discussion of generosity or lack of it on the job is complete without some consideration of the motivation behind a boss's perceived cheapness. As in any relationship, an attempt to understand the other person is often the key ingredient to a successful relationship. I once heard a young employee say, "My boss lived through the Great Depression, and as a result, he's really a hard man with a buck." That boss's wife, having survived the same experience, responded that her husband just had a long memory of the lean years of the Depression era and didn't spend money frivolously.

There is a significant difference between a boss who makes $200,000 a year and asks the employee to buy coffee for the office and one who lives a frugal life. In the latter case, the boss is consistent and indeed imposing the same rules on himself as he imposes on his employees. It's hard to find fault with a person who treats the employee the same way he treats himself. You might not wish to continue to work for such a person, but his position is understandable. You can disagree with him, but you really can't blame him. On the other hand, a boss like the one who treats himself to a splendid lifestyle while being a cheapskate to those who work for him is really not someone you should plan on building a career around. He needs to change his ways and learn to treasure his employees or he will have continuous turnover. He's reaping what he's sowing.

In any event, the fact remains that not all cheapskates are created equal. By understanding their motivation, you can learn to deal with the chintzy boss accordingly.

But, let's look at a couple of letters about bosses who have raised the level of being a tightwad to an art form.

Scrooge with a Medical Degree

CHEAP, CHEAP, CHEAP! I work for a tightwad doctor who earns more than two million a year. We work at least fifty hours a week, but he won't pay overtime. When we work late, he allows us to call home, but we have to put thirty cents in a box next to the phone.

We have to buy our own office supplies and pay for coffee and doughnuts. He helps himself to our morning snacks and lunches and never pays a nickel. On rare occasions, he brings in tea bags and we have to hang up the tea bags to dry, so we can get at least three cups per bag!

On the way home from work, Doc stops in the public rest rooms of our office building and helps himself to rolls of toilet paper, which he brings to our office, along with miniature soaps he collects from motels.

This penny-pincher is a multimillionaire who refuses to pay for a newspaper. He collects the ones our patients leave behind and takes them home. It's very, very difficult to work for this reincarnation of Jack Benny.

Scrooge With a Vengeance

MY INEPT, STINGY BOSS procrastinates for months about pay raises, office repairs, and credit memos. He circulated a memo threatening immediate dismissal for any employee caught adjusting the office thermostat or radio. Another memo demanded that employees taking time off for a funeral must bring in a copy of the obituary to verify their relationship to the deceased before they receive their paychecks.

He directed that the company trash be stored in our warehouse to save on collection fees, and even asked me to steal magazines and phone books from our customers to use in our office.

The final straw was when he called a 900 number for psychic advice on financial and other important decisions—right before the company went bankrupt!

These bosses obviously have missed the point. Actually, the best advice I can give to someone who works for a multimillionaire who steals toilet paper from public rest rooms or who works for a boss who seeks financial advice from a psychic is, "Be careful." Bosses like these who are so out of touch with reality may have more problems than meet the eye. Working in such an environment can be neither professionally nor personally beneficial, and I wonder why anyone would work for such a skinflint. This raises an important point.

When a boss is out of touch with reality, you can try to change him. But if that doesn't work, use your ingenuity to find another job. There are plenty of generous bosses out there looking for good employees, such as the following.

Santa with a Vision

JOHN IS THE MOST UNSELFISH BOSS I know. He not only pays fully for his employee's health insurance coverage, but also for our dependent coverage. Employees wishing to further their education have their college courses paid for, as well as their books and any other expenses. Most importantly, we are allowed to attend courses during company time while being paid full salary.

He generously promotes "family" by providing two months' paid maternity leave and sends flowers to us or our family members when we're hospitalized. It's not only the big things that my boss believes in doing for his employees, but it's the little things that mean a great deal to us. No one's birthday goes unnoticed without a card, cake, and small gift. Every year our firm sponsors a picnic and a Christmas party and gives generously to local charities.

He helps the needy by sponsoring twenty-five kids in the

Red Cross "Letters to Santa" program. He also buys one thousand dollars in toys each Christmas for the Toys for Tots program.

Santa at Home and Work

JERRY MOTIVATES EMPLOYEES by being the most giving, caring, and understanding person we've ever met. He has a very generous profit sharing and pension plan in action, as well as a 401(K) program. Also, he reimburses us all out-of-pocket medical expenses up to two thousand dollars each year.

He has taken us and our spouses on a company trip every year. We've been to the Bahamas, Hawaii, Cancun, and Lake Tahoe. Generous almost to a fault, he is happiest when he is doing something for or giving things to others. We are invited to use his beautiful lake home, ski boat, and fishing boat, as well as his home in Florida when any of us visit Disney World. The first day that Disney's Lion King was released on video, he bought every employee a copy. Many times he has sent the girls in the office to a spa for the day and sent the guys on a golf outing.

When we moved our office to another city, the assistant manager, myself, and a new employee borrowed money from him so we could afford to buy houses in the area. He also has helped most of the employees to buy houses, cars, boats, land, etc.

Another example of his commitment to his employees was during my recent family tragedy. My brother-in-law, who served in the Navy, was lost at sea. During perhaps the most difficult time I have ever experienced, he granted me as much personal leave as I desired, as well as emotional strength and support. One of the largest individual donations to the widow and her children was given by my boss!

Now, aren't these great bosses? Anyone would like to work for one of them. That's the problem. Kind and generous bosses can take the pick of the crop. So if you want to work for one, you'd better be the best you can be at your job. It's worth the hard work to get a job with a great boss if you can, but it seldom just happens. You may need to try to get your present boss to change his or her penny-pinching behavior. After all, it's not impossible.

The Corporate Coach's Comments

It is entirely possible that the boss you consider too cheap considers himself to be generous, kind, and sharing. Therefore, I recommend a three-step process.

The first step is to assess fairly five or ten things the boss has done that you think make him a cheapskate. Discuss them with close friends (*not fellow workers!*) and try to determine if it is indeed the boss's spending habits that are out of whack.

If you believe that you objectively have determined that the boss is a skinflint, think about why. Did he come from a meager upbringing? Has he suffered previous business reversals and is just being careful? Does he live his whole life frugally? Does he treat himself as he treats his employees?

Now, if you find that he treats his employees poorly because of his cheapness and he has no reason for doing so, you must then decide if the cheapness so affects your personal and professional development that you cannot continue to work for him. If so, list the points that you feel are issues of unacceptable cheapness and prepare for a meeting with the boss.

Of course, bosses are still bosses, so it is always best to set an appointment and ask the boss if you can have a few moments of his time. Open the meeting with an acknowledgment that you understand the importance of profitability to the company. Tell him that you believe there are a few areas where the company may be "*penny-wise and pound-foolish*" and that you can recommend some ways by which the company actually could make more money by spending a few dollars. Give concrete recommendations.

For example, it may make sense to raise the starting salary of a clerk to avoid having to retrain a new employee every two months when a better offer comes to the first employee.

REMEMBER, cheap bosses who are "treatable" are really just trying to make more money for the company. If you can show them how being a bit more "generous" might help do that, your advice might be gladly accepted.

REMEMBER, only the very best bosses are able to understand things from the perspective of even the lowest-grade employee. He truly may not realize that he is hurting the company by his cheapness. He may appreciate the perspective you bring.

If, on the other hand, he's cheap and he has no reason for it, and he is unwilling to adjust for his own or the employee's good, remember that an employee can seek greener pastures and should do so in such a case.

Coach's Corner

TO THE EMPLOYEE:

☛ Determine whether the boss is *really cheap* or just not as generous as you would hope.

☛ Try to understand *why* a boss is cheap before you condemn.

☛ Think about the difference between being cheap versus just being a responsible manager of company property.

☛ Decide whether the boss's cheapness is an inconvenience or something you just can't tolerate on a daily basis.

☛ Consider having a logical discussion with the boss about how loosening the purse strings of the company could actually make it more profitable.

TO THE BOSS:

☛ Consider whether you share fairly the rewards of the business with those who help you succeed.

☛ Weigh the expense of cost-cutting measures against bottom-line profitability.

☛ Keep your eyes and ears open to employees who point out unreasonable cost management practices.

☛ Try to understand cost cuts from the employees' point of view—walk a mile in their shoes.

CHAPTER 2

Dictators and Humanitarians

HAVE YOU EVER HEARD THESE EXPRESSIONS used to describe the business world?

- *It's a jungle out there.*
- *If you can't stand the heat, get out of the kitchen.*
- *It's a dog-eat-dog world.*
- *Every man for himself.*
- *It's kill or be killed.*

The Corporate Coach asks just one question: *Does it have to be this way?* Why should business have to be this way? Based on my years of experience, I can assure you that it doesn't have to be. There are many corporate environments in which companies, their bosses and employees all thrive and coexist in peace. They compete successfully without taking up a sword and heading into battle every day as if their business world was some type of battleground.

In this area, as in so many others, the boss sets the tone for the company. If he sees business as a war, it will be. And every employee who works for him will be treated like a soldier. If, on the other hand, the boss believes in the theory of a *win-win* business world in which there is always room for greater success, his employees and the company will be successful.

You've heard the "jungle out there" stuff way too often. That's why we have some bosses (and employees) who make going to work like going to war. I believe that *if you enjoy your job, you never have to go to work!* And it's mighty tough to enjoy your job when battle lines are drawn and when folks think of their jobs as "me against you" and "us against them."

If the boss sees the business world as a win-lose proposition, he will use all of the competitive weapons he has to offer—and he'll expect you to do the same. That's where the boss sets the tone of the business—win at all costs...the end justifies the means...if I give you a break, you'll turn around and use it to beat me...and so on. But, if the boss sees the world as a win-win opportunity, he is far more likely to add a good measure of compassion in his dealings with both employees and his competition. And in my experience in over thirty-five years of competing in business, kindness, compassion, and cooperation yield more long-term fruits than cutthroat tactics ever will.

Now, I'm not Pollyannaish. The world isn't all sugar and spice. But it is possible to compete and prosper by using your wits and your willingness to work...tempered with a liberal dose of compassion. Remember chapter 1, "Scrooges and Santas"? In that chapter, we proved that spending a few extra bucks can often actually yield more long-term profit than squeezing every penny. Remember all of that toilet paper we were able to buy? The same principle applies here. Work hard and compete hard, but by adding a touch of compassion, you might make more money in business than by being the cold-hearted dictator who still believes in the "kill or be killed" theory of business.

If you treat people fairly, they'll treat you fairly. And vice versa. In the long run, a little kindness almost always will result in greater success.

Now look at a few excerpts from employees whose hard-hearted bosses view long term as five o'clock in the afternoon.

AN ELDERLY ENGINEER in our office passed away at his desk at approximately three o'clock. My boss, the "paragon of virtue," told us not to call 911 until five o'clock because it would disrupt the routine and be nonproductive.

～

MY FATHER DIED unexpectedly last summer. Two weeks after the funeral my boss called me into his office and said,

"You need to smile and laugh more. Leave your grief at home between eight o'clock and five o'clock." One month later my grandmother died, and I wasn't even permitted to take time off work to attend her funeral. He lacks even the most basic human levels of compassion. When my brother-in-law was almost killed in an industrial accident, I took two days of my own vacation to stay at his bedside with my sister. Waiting for me on my answering machine when I returned from an all-day hospital vigil was my boss's voice, "There is nothing you can do to help him and there is work to be done here...get back to the office!"

∾

HIS MANAGEMENT STYLE of pure intimidation was particularly obvious on Saturdays, which were our biggest sales day, as home builders. He would rummage through our desks and, if he found anything out of perfect order, he would dump the drawers in the middle of the floor. If an office plant had a single brown leaf, he would pick it up and throw it out the front door, spilling dirt all over the front walk and expect us to clean up the mess. On rainy days, he would single me out to go outside in the rain to put up the flags on the flagpoles, which left my hair and clothes soaking for the day.

∾

MY BOSS IS THE WORST DICTATOR! He once felt he had discarded some very important papers by mistake and made the receptionist climb into our trash dumpster to locate the missing papers. She emerged covered with dog droppings, garbage from the hamburger joint next door, and other unidentifiable refuse...but never found the papers. They were in his briefcase at home!

∾

ONCE MY BOSS FORCED ME to take elderly residents in our rest home on an outing, knowing that the bus had a severe mechanical problem. When we were stranded on a highway in ninety-degree heat, his reaction was, "These people are eighty years old. What are their lives worth anyway?"

~

SOME DICTATORS GET AN EARLY START in life and begin
their overpowering need to control the smallest and easiest
targets–children. Our principal demanded that students
hold their lunch trays in their left hand and scrape remaining food off with their forks in right hands...pretty tricky
for five- and six-year-olds. She once got nose-to-nose with
an eight-year-old girl, who was trembling and trying to
explain the reason she sold Girl Scout cookies to her mother's teacher friend. She screamed through gritted teeth,
"This is MY school and I won't have it. Do you understand
that?" When one of the secretaries received a box of candy
as a "thank you" from the photographer for her help with
school pictures, the principal grabbed it from her hands
and said, "You'll get this when I'm ready to give it to you!"

These coldhearted bosses have yet to learn the lesson that you
can be effective without being harsh. Take the boss who didn't
show concern for the employee whose relative had died. If that
employee had a chance to move to a different company that
cared about its employees, do you think he would be concerned
if his leaving hurt the company? On the other hand, if a boss
shows compassion in his dealings with employees, generally the
employees will return that kindness.

Many times we've had employees in our companies move on
to new opportunities. We wish them well in their new jobs. But
I'm always pleased when I hear them offer to come in on nights
and weekends to help train their replacements and make certain
that the transition goes well. Do you think that an employee
would do this for a boss who makes him dig in the dumpster for
his mislaid papers?

While we're at it, let me make another point. Bosses sometimes don't give their employees credit for having eyes and a
brain. They forget that the people who work for them see every
coldhearted thing that the boss does. They understand what he's
made of. And they also recognize that if push comes to shove,
the boss will treat them in exactly the same way he has treated
others. Think about the letter regarding the dead engineer. Every
employee who knew that the coworker was left dead in his office

could picture himself being treated in the same way. Every person who knew that the boss sent the employee out on the road with elderly patients in a rickety old bus knew that the boss wouldn't hesitate putting him in a dangerous situation if it suited the boss's needs.

Despite financial necessity, it's difficult to imagine why anyone would endure such inhumanity and cruelty from a boss like those described in the examples in this chapter. I know I wouldn't. Isn't it reassuring, however, to know that there are bosses who are successful in their work without acting like Attila the Hun. They have taken to heart the saying, "You catch more flies with honey than vinegar."

Let's look at a few examples from employees working for bosses who understand this old saying.

BEING THE SINGLE PARENT of a fifteen-year-old daughter and having no family in the area has meant my having to leave work at odd times for orthodontist, doctor, and school appointments. My boss is always understanding and insists that my family comes first. Although David has been an amputee from childhood bouts with cancer, he runs his company with compassion, strength of purpose, and strength of character.

∼

WHEN MY FATHER-IN-LAW WAS ILL, my boss Dianna baked his favorite candy. She also baked me a huge plate of goodies at Christmas! She helped throw a shower when I went on maternity leave and put no pressure on me about coming back. In fact she insisted that I not return to my full schedule for some time. After the baby arrived, I was hesitant about leaving my new daughter (who was sick) with our young baby-sitter. It was Dianna who insisted on baby-sitting—and that wasn't the first time! She constantly looked for new and improved techniques or equipment to protect her employees.

∼

DURING A FAMILY EMERGENCY, my boss told me to leave at once. Bob also gave me peace of mind by saying, "When you get to Heaven, God won't ask you what you

did for the corporation. He will ask you what you did for
your family."

∾

I HAD WORKED FOR A WONDERFUL DENTIST for eleven
months and was about to celebrate my first wedding
anniversary when my husband received orders to go over-
seas for two years without me. I was devastated when he
left. My boss asked me, "How much would a one-way ticket
cost to London?" I told him I didn't have any idea and only
knew I couldn't afford it. The next payday, he wrote me a
check to move my household to England. I'll never forget
his kindness as he told me, "Families should be together."
Thanks to him I had the opportunity to live in England
with my husband and to travel throughout Europe.

∾

CHUCK ENCOURAGES MORNING MEETINGS, often
bringing doughnuts, where we can discuss business or personal problems and items of interest. He handles problems
and problem people with grace and humor. He acknowl-
edges employee birthdays, Secretary's Day, and even baby
showers with thoughtful cards and generous gifts. For my
birthday he called eight restaurants to locate one that
served veal picatta, after I mentioned that I hadn't had the
dish for a long time. He allows me to work a very flexible
schedule in order to coordinate with my mother's job, so
that she can provide child care for my children.

∾

HIS DAYS ARE FILLED with never-ending phone calls, constant deadlines, and numerous problem-solving challenges.
Nonetheless, he finds time to send his own faxes, make his
own copies, get his own coffee, and answer his own phone
because he knows my schedule is just as hectic. No ego
problem here! If we've had a hectic week, it's not unusual
for him to say, "Why don't you leave early today, we've
had a really rough week." I have two small children and
Brian is flexible with my work schedule because I'm some-

times pulled away for slashed fingers, high fevers, and upset stomachs. He has never made me feel guilty for my absence or disruption of his day. In fact he encourages me to put family first, to volunteer for my son's field trips, and take early or late lunches to attend school plays.

I think we would agree that the common thread connecting each of these bosses is their compassion, personal involvement, and concern for their employees. Their creativity and the variety of avenues used to build relationships based on trust and loyalty should set the standard for any manager to emulate. Unquestionably, each of them has discovered the secret to making their staff feel important—treat them like *part of the family*. And how do they do that? Why not try some of their ideas. For example:

Create flex time for families.
Provide welcome baskets.
Send birthday cards.
Send employee to London to be with family if you can afford it.
Bake some special treats.

Now there can be no question as to the kindness of the boss who sent the woman to be with her husband in England. Wow! That's great and very generous, but not everyone can afford such grand gestures. So don't worry about the big, generous acts of kindness. Think of the thousand little things you can do each day to show compassion. Think of the boss who made a batch of candy, or the one who filled in as a baby-sitter in a pinch. These were terrific helps to the people involved, and they cost very little. But many times, the acts of kindness and small expenditures are secondary to what people crave most—support and encouragement.

The Extended Family From Nine to Five

The traditional family unit provides emotional support, love, and encouragement. But because of the rapid rise in the number of divorces, single parent families, commuter marriages, and the like, our families are often not traditional. Yet, even in traditional homes, employees spend more waking hours with coworkers than they do with their families. Let's look at the numbers:

Based on a Five-Day Work Week (Monday-Friday)

24 hours x 5 =	120 hours
Less:	
Time at work: 9 hours (including lunch) per day x 5 days	45 hours
Commute to and from the job:	5 hours
Hours of sleep: 8 hours per night (Monday-Friday)	40 hours
Hours left for family (Monday-Friday)	30 hours

Even if you spent 100 percent of your free time with your family, it barely would be more than the time most of us spend at our jobs. So it stands to reason that the time together at work should be as enjoyable and fulfilling as possible.

This can be done in a variety of ways. Bosses can show a personal interest in employees and what they are interested in. At performance review time, they can check on progress the employees are making on their personal, as well as professional goals.

A work family should give a sense of caring and belonging to all its members. Unfortunately, the following letters depict cold and dominating bosses who haven't made an investment in the personal lives of their employees.

The Führer Reigns

ONE OF MY COWORKERS had been missing for three days when my boss learned early in the morning that she had been found dead. He wouldn't tell any of the employees that our anxious days were over until we were ready to leave for the day. He didn't want our sales volume to be affected, if we were upset, so that we wouldn't be able to put in a full eight hours for him. He immediately removed the deceased employee from our company insurance to save on the premiums because he didn't feel her family needed the death benefit check. After all, the beneficiary was a doctor!

He insisted that an employee contact her father's surgeon

and delay her eighty-five-year-old father's surgery so the
employee wouldn't have to miss a day of work.

When an employee suffered a heart attack at his desk,
our boss made coworkers go back to work instead of helping. He wanted to see the disgusted looks on the para-
medics' faces!

He discovered that some of his salespeople sell better
when they are high on alcohol or drugs, so he gave cash
advances for them to buy whatever they needed to keep
sales figures up, just as long as they came back to work!

He's Heavy—and He's Not My Brother

IN THE RAPIDLY CHANGING WORLD of telemarket-
ing, it's really hard to stay focused and on your toes
when you always have someone on your back! My
boss would start our weekly sales meetings by throwing a phone or a chair to get everyone's attention. Although
he was only five foot three inches tall and about 135 pounds
soaking wet, he would sometimes punch a door just to let
everyone know how much power he had within the company. Wearing black, he would stroll through the office, saying
that he was in a bad mood and was going to fire someone,
which he did almost daily. In fact in a period of three days,
he fired twelve people. One employee was singled out and
fired because he walked with a limp.

He would make grown men wear dunce caps for not
saying the right things on the phone. We spoke from his
strict text with no latitude for personal comments on a specific sales call. He allowed only his wording and expressions—our phrases were strictly forbidden.

He once told a sixty-two-year-old man, who had just discovered he had cancer, to hurry up and die so he could put
another person at his desk. The employee died only two
months later.

These are sad examples of people who have forgotten that their
employees are people with emotions and feelings. It's impossible
to imagine how they expect their employees to give 100 percent
(or 50 percent, for that matter) for a boss who is so coldhearted
and dictatorial.

Compare these bosses to those described in the letters below.

He Lives by the Golden Rule

DON'S PHILOSOPHY is to treat others the way he wants to be treated, to be fair and honest. He encourages his employees to make time for family and provides for time off for family. He advocates a positive attitude, so he has nurtured and motivated us as individuals to be more productive. Don provides the usual employee benefits, as well as educational seminars and praise for our accomplishments.

In 1995, my husband was diagnosed with terminal, inoperable cancer and given six months to live. Don jumped to the forefront and encouraged me to stay at my husband's bedside. He and his wife and the staff were there for me and work was put on hold. Staff members provided food, housework, and a cellular phone. He even offered airline tickets for relatives beginning to assemble during my husband's last days.

We prayed together and cried together. His wife was one of many at my husband's bedside when the call came that my father had suffered a massive heart attack and died. Don made airline reservations for my trip home for Dad's funeral and paid the expenses. On Easter Sunday my husband died, and Don nurtured me through my husband's funeral. His business closed the day of the funeral and he provided a beautiful reception afterward at his home.

Charity Does Begin in the Heart

BILL HAS BEEN A COACH, a mentor, and a true leader; and he definitely makes Easter Seal a great place to work! He allows "great people to become outstanding and outstanding people to become even more tremendous."

He brings breakfast and cakes to each one of our three centers monthly to give people a chance to talk with him about any issues, concerns, or celebrations–or just to talk.

Once a month, Bill spends the entire day as an aide in our therapy area to better understand the challenges of our team and of the children who are patients there. He's right there–listening, learning, and helping.

Thoughtfully, he dresses like a clown at children's parties at our centers and sends birthday cards to every child, every team member, and every board member (and even to our spouses).

Perhaps Bill's most unique managerial inspiration is that he conducts quarterly appraisals on himself–and wants to know how he can do better!

Compassion, motivation, generosity, friendship–who could ask for more? These bosses have solved the puzzle of employee motivation and morale. They have understood that the job doesn't have to be a win-lose proposition and that kindness and compassion are two of the greatest keys to success in the business world.

The Corporate Coach's Comments

It's difficult to tell a boss that he is coldhearted. The reason is because there is really no objective measure of kindness or cruelty. What I consider unbearably cruel, another person might think of as fair and reasonable. So my first advice is to go slowly.

The first thing to do is to try to be as fair as you can. We all tend to look for evidence to prove whatever point we want to make. In other words, we sometimes are guilty of trying to make the evidence create the crime. So make sure that you're not guilty of that before going any further. If you are convinced, however, that the boss is really a dyed-in-the-wool, real-life, coldhearted person, I suggest the following approach.

Make an appointment to talk to your boss and tell him that you have a problem and you would really like his advice on it. Remember now, coldheartedness is not a crime. Therefore, you can't marshal your facts in this case and overwhelm the boss with your evidence! Tell the boss that you are having problems with the way the company (not the boss!) is dealing with certain people or situations. Then say that you realize it's probably your problem, because you may be too sensitive or softhearted. However, you fear that in today's business environment others may have the same impression—even if it is wrong—that you have, and you would hate to see the company get in trouble for the sake of impressions.

Suggest that maybe a little more kid-glove treatment would be in order to assure that everybody can keep focused on work and hurt feelings can be kept to a minimum. Again, appeal to the fact that it's in the best financial interest of the company (and the boss) to keep employees motivated and feeling appreciated.

This medicine may take multiple doses—and it simply may fall on deaf ears. On the other hand your advice, properly given, may raise the level of the boss's sensitivity just a bit and create a better work environment for you, your coworkers, and even your boss.

Coach's Corner

TO THE EMPLOYEE:

☞ Try to understand what events in your boss's background might have contributed to his or her need to dominate people and rule with an iron fist.

☞ Decide if your job is worth the risk of taking on a dictatorial boss to try to soften his demeanor. If so, set about establishing your game plan, on a professional basis, and "go for it."

☞ Forget past injustices and leave your bitterness at the boss's office door before you enter. Dwell on positive solutions to the problems at hand.

☞ Differentiate between a dyed-in-the-wool, real-life dictator and a boss "just having a bad day."

☞ Never allow a boss to take away your dignity and self-respect.

☞ Treat your coworkers as you would treat your family. You almost spend more time on the job than you do with your family.

TO THE BOSS:

☞ Remember, for you to succeed, someone else doesn't have to fail. There's plenty of opportunity to go around.

☞ Be aware that the boss sets the stage for others. If you're tough and cold, your employees are likely to be also.

☞ Be kind, because it seldom costs much and it pays huge dividends.

☞ Let employees know you are interested in them as people. This is critical to creating a positive work environment.

☞ Conduct meetings in less formal environments to open channels of communication.

☞ Create an "extended family" atmosphere for employees at work.

☞ Bear in mind you can catch more flies with honey than with vinegar.

CHAPTER 3

Big Brothers and Believers

He orchestrated a network of spies, placed strategically throughout the school. As principal, he monitored all the rooms through the public address system. He was a master at stimulating fear and dissent in the staff and introduced himself as "The Bear"...because "a Big Bear goes anywhere it wants to."

IN A COUNTRY where privacy is almost sacredly protected by our legal system, it amazed me that we received letter after letter in our annual contest telling of bosses who went to unbelievable lengths to snoop on their employees. They installed listening and surveillance devices throughout their facilities. Some sneaky bosses even left the premises and returned secretly to spy on employees from a closet, routinely opened employees' personal mail, eavesdropped on business and personal phone calls, and frequently searched through employees' purses, lockers, and wastebaskets.

These bosses weren't just being careful. Too often it went way beyond that. These folks were more interested in playing 007 with their employees' lives than they were with taking care of business. Business is tough enough if everyone is working together, and it's downright impossible if you spend 75 percent of your time looking over your shoulder and covering your backside.

Whether it is a result of uncertainty about employees' abilities or loyalty, insecurity in their own competence or job knowledge—or just plain paranoia—these bosses create a living nightmare for their employees.

When you read some of the following excerpts, I think you will feel as revolted as I did about employees being victimized, controlled, and scrutinized as Big Brother watched.

BIG BROTHER IS AT MY COMPANY. My boss has installed cameras throughout the office and listening devices on the telephones. You never know when he may be watching or recording your every move.

～

OUR CORPORATE ROACH considers each employee's desk his business. While I'm away from my desk, he feels free to rummage through my desk at will. If he finds something worth commenting on, he leaves a note. Nobody at the company is exempt from his antics. For example, our vice president decided to retire after seventeen years of building the company and the day before his retirement party, the "Roach" fired him over a disagreement concerning his final paycheck.

～

MY BOSS practiced the J. Edgar Hoover style of management. He searched the offices of his subordinates during off hours. Memos, files, and phone messages would disappear and suddenly reappear in his hands. He interviewed former employees, for additional "dirt" for his files. No offense was too small to merit notation. I personally was "noted" for rolling my eyes at a meeting, having a typo in a letter, and going to lunch with a manager who happened to be gay. Oh yes, all this information went into secret files he kept under lock and key.

～

IT WAS NOT UNUSUAL to walk out of my office and literally fall on top of my boss, as he sat on the floor listening to personal phone calls or private conversations. He used this tactic to find fault with people he wanted to terminate. He made it clear that he wanted only employees who "needed their paycheck," so he held checks until after lunch to see how many would go to lunch before he distributed paychecks.

~

AN ARROGANT EGOMANIAC, our boss loves to search employees' desks when they leave the office and open their personal mail, if it comes to the office by mistake. As he struts around the office enjoying his power trip, he browbeats and belittles employees with comments like, "This office belongs to me, without exception, and the employee has no rights whatsoever to complain or protest."

~

MY BOSS'S TECHNIQUE is relentless. He plants spies on all committees and owns all the committees. He monitors mailboxes and phone calls. He keeps track of his (perceived) enemies' movements. He trains his followers to detect and report any suspicious and critical behavior so he can stomp out any hint of dissent.

~

IF INSECURITY IS A LESSER FORM OF PARANOIA, then my boss qualified for both the lesser and greater of the two evils. She hid in the rest room, sitting on the toilet to balance her checkbook. She began to stay home "sick" but would return late at night to ransack offices, even going through the garbage. When she would come in during office hours, she prowled the halls, peering into offices in the belief conspiracies were afoot. She promised one staff member a raise to spy on others and gave another "special projects," like liberal leave and travel to win her loyalty.

Can you picture a boss with his or her ear plastered to a door, listening to personal conversations? I must admit, I struggled with the letters regarding these invasions of privacy. Whether we are dealing with a general lack of confidence in employees' abilities and loyalty or a case of personal insecurity, bosses who feel compelled to spy, snoop, and sneak around definitely have a problem. These bosses waste a lot of time, energy, and money in the pursuit of the uncertainty. What could be or would be happening if they weren't monitoring everything. That same time, energy, and money could be put to use elsewhere in the company to produce a trusting environment in which employees could relax and do their jobs–not look over their shoulders at Big Brother watching them.

For these bosses, the problem is simply a lack of trust. Failure to trust is, unfortunately, a course taught to some at the "school of hard knocks." In other words, some of these bosses have been burned and simply have lost their ability to trust others. However, violating the privacy of another is not the right answer. Believe me, it is much, much better for bosses who have learned that not everyone can be trusted to use the direct approach. Instead of the cloak-and-dagger routine of bugging phones, reading garbage, and searching employees' purses and lockers, suspicious bosses need to learn to confront these problems directly and squarely.

Playing With Matches

The problem some bosses have in trusting people is that they've been burned before. The pain might have been caused simply by a secretary cutting out early when the boss leaves the office for an afternoon appointment, or a manager taking care of personal busniess on company time. Or maybe it was more serious, like a cashier stealing money from the till...a salesman cheating on his expense account...a peer pulling a coup d'etat with management...or the accountant "doctoring" the company books. Whatever caused the blaze, some bosses never take a chance to trust again because they are afraid the embers will rekindle. They won't trust anyone, anywhere, any time. Now that's sad, because the majority of employees whom I've encountered over the years are honest, hardworking people.

Even more unfortunate is the negative message sent about the boss and the employees when customers and suppliers realize management feels surveillance is required at the company they do business with. What must they think of employees who can't be trusted to carry out routine responsibilities without being monitored? What must they think of bosses who continue to employ people who can't be trusted? This is a public relations nightmare. I think I would be tempted to do business elsewhere. Wouldn't you wonder how long such a company will be in business?

Check the "Twitch in Your Left Elbow"

Every human resource manager has a formula to select prospective employees. Our company is no exception, but I also rely on the "twitch in my left elbow." Some people call it "gut feelings" or "a sixth sense." The concepts are much the same. To a large degree, we rely on our physical reaction to the people we interview, as well as the sophisticated screening processes. We don't disregard numerous interviews, personality profiles, skill testing, and the like. But when comparing two shiny red apples that look alike on the surface at a fruit counter, we often resort to a hunch before putting the fruit into a sack.

Whatever process you use, the goal should be the same—hire winners who have a "can do/will do/enjoy a challenge" attitude. Despite an attractive exterior or polished resumé, run as fast as you can from someone with a "what's in it for me/it can't be done" approach to life. Set your targets on *winners,* not *losers!* When you do, three things happen. First, *trust* in your employees comes easier. Then, *confidence* in their loyalty and abilities naturally follows. And third, *dependence* on your team evolves to form a working climate that warms everyone and burns no one. Consider for a minute the differences between winners and losers:

Winner vs. Loser

The winner is part of the answer.
The loser is part of the problem.

The winner has a program.
The loser has an excuse.

The winner says, "Let me do it for you."
The loser says, "That's not my job."

The winner sees an answer in every problem.
The loser sees a problem in every answer.

The winner sees a green near every sand trap.
The loser sees two or three sand traps near every green.

The winner says, "It may be difficult, but it's not impossible."
The loser says, "It may be possible, but it's difficult."

—Anonymous

The bosses described below may or may not have resorted to a "twitch in their left elbow." Whatever method they used, the result is evident–there is open communication between their employees and themselves. When we read these letters about bosses who advocate an "open door" policy, we read about bosses who trust, have confidence, and depend on their employees. Listen to what their employees think about this philosophy.

OUR BOSS, Louie, doesn't have a hidden agenda! He keeps me involved in day-to-day activities, as well as strategic planning. He copies me on senior management and executive reports, business planning documents, and solicits my input on impending high-level, critical business decisions, such as the direction of the department and factory. I'm treated like an important part of the organization, and no matter how good I make him look, he makes me look even better.

∿

YOU CAN HEAR JANIS WHISTLING or laughing in her office throughout the day. She makes us feel good about ourselves and our accomplishments. She makes sure that we are adequately informed about all pertinent issues at work and holds frequent staff meetings to keep us updated. This gives us confidence and security about what is going on in the office. When an employee has something to say, Janis's door is always open. She realized a recent stressful project left us all a little edgy, so she announced the next day…Wednesday, a workday…she would drive us to spend the day relaxing on the deck of her beach house. We were served a delicious crab salad and refreshing drinks with fruit slices. What a wonderful day of therapy for us all.

∿

BEFORE BETH became the new strong right arm of our CEO, lines of communication were difficult between employees and administration. As a powerful advocate for dialogue with employees and management, at her urging, semiannual open meetings are held with staff, and communication now flows like water. She also initiated a recognition program to generate creative thank-you's, as well as multirater feedback surveys to supplement performance evaluations.

~

JERRY ALWAYS IS AVAILABLE to all his employees regardless of whether the issue is small or large, professional or personal, serious or playful. He will take your phone call at work, at home, or on vacation, if possible, or return your call within a few hours maximum. An employee never needs to prequalify with Jerry to see if they are worthy of his attention.

~

AUDLEY IS A TRUE ROLE MODEL, mentor, and leader. He holds daily meetings with his supervisors on three different shifts. He sets this time aside to listen to the issues and challenges faced by each supervisor. He offers assistance but leaves the responsibility of handling the issues to his supervisors. Audley also encourages cross training among the supervisors to create a more flexible department. Beneath his polished executive exterior, he is a fighter, fighting for the rights of those aren't able to fight for themselves and fighting to bring economic opportunities to those low-income citizens of our community who have been left out for so long.

~

MIKE MAKES IT CLEAR that he is no different from other employees, but just has different responsibilities. He maintains an open team spirit, communicating in staff meetings that it's the people who do the work, he's just there to help. He keeps all employees up-to-date after regional staff meetings. He infuses our meetings with "brain games" that stimulate creative flow, contribute to the open team cooperation, and uphold mental alertness. His memos are openly addressed to "Friends," instead of using impersonal formalities such as "Staff."

These letters are only a sampling of those we received about bosses who have created an atmosphere in the workplace of open communications based on trust, confidence, and a team spirit. It's obvious that employees enjoy and thrive in such an environment. It follows naturally that, when people feel important and good about themselves, they are happier, more productive workers.

Give Them Their Say, Not Necessarily Their Way

We've seen that the real antidote for distrust and spying is open communication. This doesn't mean that bosses have to be pushovers. It does mean that they have to listen. Keeping the lines of communication open is critical to any successful company. Bear in mind, however, that feedback can be both positive and negative. Regardless, it's important that management allows employees to express their opinions—to have their say. And frustrated, angry people will have their say. If not, they will explode and tell everyone around about their problem. And this eruption will splatter over onto customers just as easily as it will spill onto coworkers.

Furnishing a platform for workers to voice opinions doesn't require building an elaborate soapbox. Nor does constructing a system to let them have their say—good or bad—necessarily mean that they will have their way. It does enable managers to create programs that will allow people to vent their feelings before it becomes obvious that a problem exists and a boss is tempted to go "undercover" to figure out what's going on.

A word of caution here to employees: Even with the most understanding boss at the helm and very sophisticated feedback programs in place, there are times when the response to your suggestions and ideas will be "No." There may be things going on beyond your knowledge that cause the boss's response to be "No" when you're hoping for a "Yes." So don't condemn the communication process just because it didn't produce the answer you wanted.

A word of caution to bosses: When you open the feedback floodgates, you must be prepared for the deluge to follow. It may come in a trickle at first, but when word filters down that their input is earnestly sought, employees will begin to participate. Then the challenge really begins. Bosses must *listen, be flexible and responsive* to not only their employees' ideas and suggestions, but also to their frustrations and occasional "ax grindings."

Tapping Your Inner Sources

Employee suggestion programs are a logical place to start bridging the boss-employee communication gap without resorting to James Bond tactics. A company can benefit from a variety of feedback programs. Systematic employee involvement teams bring day-to-day operational problems to the attention of management—most often with corrective suggestions. Quality-emphasis programs, particularly those that are team-driven, reduce errors and expense and add to the bottom-line profitability of the company. Departmental and interdepartmental meetings promote an understanding and appreciation of one another's area of responsibilities. Bottom-up strategic planning provides employee input from every level within the company prior to corporate annual meetings. Whatever vehicle is used, feedback is feedback.

Still, the easiest and best source of information continues to be the *annual employee opinion survey.* When this is administered by an outside agency, employees can be assured of confidentiality and, thus, be candid in their remarks. To get the full story, a survey should provide space for employees to write at length about issues—positive or negative—not covered in the "check the appropriate box" sections. It's amazing to see the light shed in some dark areas of the company by the survey results. Managers can spot trouble within and between departments, not obvious on the surface. A difficult employee, or manager for that matter, can be identified and dealt with to bring harmony back to the team. Employees will provide input on procedures, benefits, training, working environment, and so forth. There is no boundary for employees when they discuss their working environment. And, after all, the workplace is our area of concern here.

It's somewhat like a reflection in a mirror. The image given is the image received. How the boss relates to employees—good or bad—is pretty much how employees relate to the boss. The reflections are obvious in the four following letters. The first two look in the mirror and gaze at the images in the background. They are watching their backs and don't grasp their own image. The second two bosses look in the mirror to see how well their employees are performing in a trusting atmosphere.

Quiet! Big Brother's Listening In the Closet

HE MANAGES BY IRRITATION! After saying his "good nights" to the office, our boss would leave around three o'clock in the afternoon. He then would return by sneaking up the back stairway. Ever so quietly, he would unlock the supply closet door, go inside, and close the door. For the next two hours he would stand inside the closet with the door closed and the light off listening to what employees said when they thought he was gone for the day. He also took notes on which employees left early.

Other annoying habits included his searching employees' desks and trash cans daily. When he wanted coffee or tea, he invented a bogus errand to send an employee on. Then he rushed into the employee's office and helped himself to the coffee or tea, being careful not to get caught.

He further invaded employees' privacy by watching the group's telephone switchboard. When a light would go on, indicating someone was using their phone, he would run into that employee's office to sit down and listen.

His managerial skills included barging into an employee's office without knocking whenever he saw the office door closed. When meetings were in progress, whether a visitor had dropped by, or if the employee was only eating lunch, he would rush in, sit down, intently watch and listen…and refuse to leave.

Management by Paranoia and Subordination

ALL EMPLOYEES IN OUR OFFICE were required to sign a fifty-six-page non-compete agreement, "the Bible," which stipulated it was for his entire kingdom.

Every telephone or personal conversation with our paranoid boss, or a client, was recorded. The command post, his office, had an intercom system where he would turn a switch to listen to conversations throughout the building.

Thursday nights were a big and exciting night for him.
He would extend his perimeter of surveillance from the
command post to the trash of our competitors. He was concerned that there was a conspiracy against him and was
fearful one of his employees would make contact with the
enemy. The potential defector was summoned to the command post and questioned about his/her desire to defect to
the Red Army...our competitor. Usually the subordinate,
after clutching their chest and gasping for air, would begin
to stammer and stutter. The stunned employee then was
advised they were being reassigned under direct supervision and much closer to the command post.

The two following letters picture companies where the employees
work in an open, positive environment. The Big Brother attitude
doesn't exist. I think you'll agree these two bosses make work a
pleasure.

The Messenger on a Motorcycle

OUR SCHOOL PRINCIPAL rode a motorcycle down
the hallway during teacher in-service training for a motivational effect before school started last year. What a dramatic
way to communicate, "Let's hit the road together for a great
school year!"

Bill, our effervescent principal, communicates through
newsletters, announcements, weekly agendas, phone calls,
and handwritten, personal notes. He extends an open-door
policy where he listens to concerns, complaints, and compliments. He encourages brainstorming to solve problems,
listening to and following up on recommendations.

As a leader in Texas education, Bill travels extensively to
stay abreast of innovative ideas and techniques, which he
shares with his staff. He encourages staff members to be as
politically active and involved in professional organizations as
he is.

His innovations for improved job production include giving comp time, teaching a class while giving the teacher an
"off period," taking lunch duty, awarding prizes for most

improved and highest test scores, and best attendance. When Bill won airline tickets in a contest, he gave the tickets to the teacher whose class had the greatest contest participation.

Staff members are recognized and rewarded for giving extra time to students, sponsoring after-school clubs, as well as for outstanding achievements. Under his leadership, our school has been recognized by the state for innovations and scholastic achievement.

The Caretaker with a Sense of Humor

CHUCK VIEWS HIS MANAGEMENT STYLE as taking care of the staff, so we can take care of our mentally ill and developmentally disabled patients.

He truly believes and practices that, if you give people enough knowledge, they can solve most problems. Chuck gives us the information, flexibility and authority to do our jobs. Changes are implemented slowly, so we can learn, and he elicits input from those who will be affected by his decisions.

With gentle humor, and poking fun at himself and at us, Chuck helps us keep things in perspective and interesting. For example, he writes meeting minutes in such a humorous way that we anxiously wait to grab them "hot off the copy machine" like the latest best-seller. Recently, when an idea of his was voted down, he commented, "The boss picked up his ball and bat and went home." Another meeting recap read, "lots of heads nodding in agreement like little dogs in the back of car windows."

Chuck keeps the focus on the problem to be solved, not on the personalities and politics in the office. He points out when we are whining, but never whines himself. He is a compassionate boss as he openly pushes us, kicking and protesting, into "opportunities for growth."

Well, we've covered a lot of ground in this chapter and I hope the message is clear. For whatever reason, it is never appropriate to resort to dishonest, degrading spy tactics to manage a business. If such practices are happening at your workplace, it is absolutely essential that the bosses and employees learn how to deal with problems and concerns. You'll be amazed at the productivity gains you'll enjoy when open, direct communication and employee feedback replace cloak-and-dagger games. Good luck—and turn in your trench coat and magnifying glass at the lost and found desk!

The Corporate Coach's Comments

I have a difficult time addressing the issue of spying from personal experience because it is so foreign to my way of running a company. Fortunately, I've never dealt with the spying and snooping discussed in this chapter. Unfortunately, however, the volume of letters we received indicates that this does go on in the workplace. So what do you do if your boss is up to these tricks?

Your boss may consider his Big Brother routine necessary to make the company run smoothly. Isn't that a frightening thought? It may be true, however, so it now becomes your job to help him see the light.

First, decide whether it's pure paranoia...a personality problem or whether the boss thinks that he needs to spy to manage the business. You can tell if it's pure paranoia by looking at how he deals with the rest of his life. For example, if he's got a good family life, balanced relationships with friends, etc., it's probably not paranoia. On the other hand, if he sees a traitor behind every door in every phase of his life—get out! There's no fixing him and there's no reason to hang around.

Hopefully, your boss can be found in the first category. If, on the other hand, you are suffering with a compulsive busybody who is obsessed with the adventure of planting spies, prowling the office after hours and rummaging through desks and trash cans, watching everyone on hidden cameras, listening to business and personal conversations, then you may be dealing with paranoia in the worst degree. No assurances that his employees are *with* him, not *against* him, will convince this overly suspicious boss that he doesn't have to "battle it alone." The impenetrable wall he has built around himself is too high for any employee to scale. It just may be time to pick up your tools, cut your losses, and look for a company where the communication bridge is already in place and the boss's door is always open for everyone to enter.

Coach's Corner

TO THE EMPLOYEE:

☛ Determine whether your boss is paranoid in all parts of his life or whether he simply has learned not to trust his employees.

☛ Identify areas where you can earn his trust and assure him that his employees are *with* him, not *against* him.

☛ Project a positive image of competence and integrity which will reassure him of your loyalty.

☛ Present suggestions where "debugging" would have an incontestable chain reaction in the company by lifting employees' spirits, increasing productivity, and escalating profits.

TO THE BOSS:

☛ Hire *winners* who have a "can do/will do/enjoy a challenge" attitude.

☛ Work at developing trust in employees who show their willingness to do a good, honest day's work.

☛ Develop an "open door" policy and build an ongoing line of communication with all levels of workers up and down your corporate ladder.

☛ Conduct annual employee opinion surveys to keep your hand on the pulse of your company. Make certain an outside firm administers this survey. You will be amazed how the feedback will isolate the ember of discontent before it blazes into a full-scale problem.

☛ Consider the productivity and profit gleaned from employees who are secure and who don't waste time or effort looking over their shoulder for Big Brother's scrutinizing eyes.

CHAPTER 4

Gross Gusses and Dapper Dans

AS WE STUDY THOSE AROUND US, it is increasingly obvious that we are all *creatures of habit*–each with our own peculiarities. For some of us, this means we function daily in our well-worn grooves, going about our business while attempting to offend as few as possible. For others, the personal idiosyncrasies that have become our trademarks are highly offensive to the people around us. It is this last group about whom employees wrote letter after letter. They described bosses, whose personal hygiene habits sicken even the most stouthearted.

For this reason, this chapter may be particularly difficult for the squeamish of heart–and of stomach. I know it certainly was for me! But, in a deliberation of whether or not to include this chapter, the decision was made to unmask the perpetrators because of the sheer numbers of contest entries that graphically character-ized bosses with unbelievably disgusting, repulsive hygiene habits. Our judges gagged their way through letter after letter describing inconceivable situations of grisly, nauseating behavior by anyone's standards. For this reason, I will make few comments in response to the gross vulgarities described in these letters. I merely offer my sympathy!

SHE IS LETHAL to morale and drives her employ-ees to despair! My three-hundred-fifty pound, food-gorging, gas-passing nightmare in pink polyester thunders through the door at eight o'clock each morning to begin our day of torture. After lighting a cigarette, she read the new "no smoking policy" and promptly put her cigarette out in my coffee cup! My office floor is littered with her cigarette ashes, candy wrappers, and dirty Kleenex.

∾

HE MANAGED A NATIONAL PIZZA CHAIN franchise, but I would never eat there. He let the kids dip snuff while they were at the make-table preparing the pizzas. They would put their spit cups on the shelf above the table. He never made anyone wash their aprons. He would wash the dishes with the pressure hose and never used a rag. He just let them drip dry, partially clean.

∾

ONE DAY A GROUP OF US ORDERED PIZZA for lunch, including my boss. As I began rinsing my mouth, I heard unusual movement. It was my boss peering over my cubicle to see if I had put the mouthwash in my mouth. When he realized he was noticed, he began laughing hysterically. I immediately suspected that he altered my mouthwash with something and raced to the rest room to spit it out. When I returned, he was in the process of telling those within earshot that he had urinated in my mouthwash, anticipating that I would use it as usual after eating pizza.

∾

HAVE YOU HEARD of people with chronic bad breath? My boss's problem is chronic gas. Once, our secretary was sitting in the reception area and he was talking to her. He dropped a silent bomb and just walked away. One of his favorite pasttimes is nose-picking and spreading his treasures any and everywhere! Most memorably, he once scratched the dandruff from his head into a little pile at a staff meeting—then proceeded to blow his little pile on the floor. Before we could recover from this spectacle, he removed his shoe while sitting at the head of the table at a supplier meeting, and proceeded to examine his sore toe. Most remarkably, he calls himself "studmuffin."

∾

MY EX-BOSS WAS THE WORST on the planet. He picked his nose and then indulged in whatever snacks you had on your desk. With no manners at all, he cut wind constantly when you were talking with him. He used the ladies' room constantly so he didn't stink up the men's room.

~

DESPITE BEING A MILLIONAIRE, my boss wears manure-stained overalls and a dirty baseball cap to work. He once asked a supervisor to hold a cup while he filled it with urine—in an airplane no less. He often asked another supervisor to pop boils on his large, sweaty body.

These were difficult excerpts to share with you, but I promised to address accurately the areas in the relationship between bosses and employees that were reported in the Worst Boss letters. The bottom line is, though, that a person who displays disgusting personal hygiene is really telling those around him that he has no respect for them. Now, to be fair, we have to remember that proper hygiene, like beauty, is subjective. However, there are basic principles that nobody would dispute. And when you're working shoulder to shoulder with others day in and day out, it's fair to ask that they conform to some standards of personal cleanliness. Those who don't are sending a message. Either they are so out of touch with reality that they don't realize their lousy habits, or they are aware and just don't care.

In either case you're dealing with a boss who has a serious problem. I don't think that any job is worth putting up with the vile habits such as those reported above. Of course, bosses aren't the only ones who are disgusting. So whether boss or employee, take a look at yourself and get yourself together—it truly is the least you can do to make your workplace a pleasant place to be.

Habits—They Make Us or Break Us

John Dryden said, "We first make our habits, and then our habits make us." During our lifetime, we accumulate thousands of habits. Most of them are good ones. Some are even necessary for our survival. For example, most of us drive a car at least once a day. As we practiced to pass our driving test eons ago, we had to stop and think as we navigated our dad's car. It didn't take long, though, for the countless actions necessary to go from point A to point B to become second nature—habits. In fact, how many times do you get in your

car, drive from one side of town to the other, arrive at your destination, and not remember the details of your trip? The same is true
of habits that we inadvertently pick up–good and bad–throughout
our life. Some habits, like turning off the closet light or locking the
back door as we leave for work, are second nature to us, and we do
those things without giving any thought to them. But it's those bad
habits–those breaches of society's acceptable behavior–that create
problems for us with our families and with the people we see from
nine to five: our coworkers and our bosses.

If a boss's behavior becomes a problem in your working relationship because of the nasty habits he's developed, and if that
behavior creates a problem with doing your job, then you have
little choice but to let the boss know how it affects you. The two
of you then can work on trying to remedy the situation. Life is too
short to live in a pigsty for most of your waking hours. But just
how do you tell someone that he's gross?

Well, the bottom line is that you've got to do it, and I suggest
an approach in the Coach's Comments at the end of this chapter.
But for now, you've got to realize that a boss's disgusting behavior reflects badly on every person who puts up with it. Some people will be asking questions like, "What sort of person puts up
with these situations?" That drags you down into the mire with
your gross boss. For better or worse, people believe the old adage
that "Birds of a feather flock together," and unless you want to be
categorized with your Gross Gus boss–tell him to clean up his
act–nicely and with discretion, of course!

Leave an "Engrossing" Impression—Not a "Gross" Reflection

When you remember an early Shirley Temple movie, what are
you thinking as your mouth forms that inevitable smile? She's
adorable, enchanting, even precocious. When you read the letters
above about nose-picking, gas-passing nightmares in the guise of
humanity, what are you thinking as your brow wrinkles and your
face forms a frown? He's disgusting, repulsive, and definitely
gross. When people think of you or your boss, what impression
crosses their mind?

Every contact we make with another human creates either a
positive, neutral, or negative result. Neutral and negative are not

good enough. Now, you can't have a positive impact each and every time you interact with someone, but you can sure try. Because people form a judgment about the way you conduct yourself personally and the way you do business with each contact, don't pass up a chance to make a good impression.

Most companies practice this philosophy in spades. They prepare in advance for interactions with the objective to make the encounters positively memorable! This applies to coworkers, customers, and bosses. I can't count the number of times I've seen someone go out of his way to escort a visitor personally to an office in our building. I hear employees' conversations throughout our building in which one person is complimenting another on a new hairstyle, an attractive outfit, or a great presentation to a customer. Employees often brush lint or a stray hair from a coworker. Before an important presentation, it's not unusual to hear reminders to bosses, "Your tie is crooked," or "Your slip is showing." It's also not unusual to see an employee stoop to pick up a piece of trash on the lawn, in the parking lot, or in the hallway at our company. The list is endless. And it all gets back to the "family thing" again. You want people who are important to you, whom you work with, or whom you work for to reflect the best image possible at all times.

The images and reflections of the bosses below speak volumes about their character and their respect for others. Do you see these bosses in your company? If not, can you make tactful suggestions and offer creative input to help replace bad habits with an image you all can take pride in?

MY BOSS RECENTLY RETIRED as president of our company, but his legacy of the highest standards of leadership, top motivator by virtue of his positive attitude, and communicator will linger for years. Gordon's daily example of dignity and respect are exemplified by the fact that, despite our sharing a private toilet, "He always put the lid down!"

∽

DELMAR CARES about his employees' financial, physical, and mental well-being at heart. New employees get a handsome black leather attaché case and, to keep us from being obsolete, he makes sure we have the latest software and training. His emphasis on neatness and appearance extends throughout the office. On top of all this, he pays well!

∽

BILL HAD A REPUTATION as being a very fussy lawyer and a little too picky. He was a meticulous dresser. With a bit of reservation, I began my job with him only to discover he was a warm, compassionate person who genuinely cares about his employees.

∽

JOHN HAS A WAY of making us feel respected and appreciated. If we stay late or make a suggestion he likes, he is quick to praise and thank us. I've never heard him raise his voice or degrade a person. If a situation between employees gets tense, he remains the calming factor. The entire company is very customer-service oriented and extremely employee oriented. We are provided with soft drinks, candy, gum, food, and condiments stocked in the refrigerator. The warehouse staff is treated to surprise lunches, doughnuts for breakfast, and even free tickets to local events. I appreciate John mostly because of his good temperament and the respect he shows to all of us. The atmosphere between coworkers is congenial and respectful and there is no back-stabbing or jealousy in his company.

∽

BILL HAS A JAR FULL OF CHOCOLATE MINTS on his desk, so that anyone can come in and grab a piece of candy– everyone from three-foot-high children to six-foot-high adults! This is his smart way to get people to be comfortable with him, and it's working daily. He brings breakfast and cakes to each of our three centers monthly and definitely makes our office a great place to work.

∽

JOHN TRULY CARES about our work and performance, but our personal lives as well. The staff often finds muffins or doughnuts in the kitchen when they arrive in the mornings.

He usually finds some kind of excuse for a staff luncheon so we can munch Chinese food or pizza together. He always is coming up with ways to make things easier and more efficient for us. And, almost unbelievably, he admits that he makes mistakes, too!

Now, these bosses really have the right idea of how to treat people. As we said before, an essential element of success is respect for others. Whether it's sharing food, running a shipshape, clean office, or whatever, it all builds working relationships.

Respect and consideration for others is truly based on one's own self-esteem. For this reason, I share with audiences around the world my favorite poem, "The Man in the Glass." The words seem so appropriate here.

The Man in the Glass

When you get what you want in your struggle for self
And the world makes you king for a day.
Just go to a mirror and look at yourself
And see what that man has to say.

For it isn't your father, mother, or wife
Whose judgment upon you must pass
The fellow whose verdict counts most in your life,
Is the one staring back from the glass.

Some people may think you are a straight-shootin' chum
And call you a wonderful guy.
But the man in the glass says you're only a bum—
If you can't look him straight in the eye.

He's the fellow to please—never mind all the rest,
For he's with you clear up to the end.
And you've passed your most dangerous, difficult test
If the man in the glass is your friend.

You may fool the whole world down the pathway of life
And get pats on your back as you pass.
But your final reward will be heartaches and tears
If you've cheated the man in the glass.

—Anonymous

From this point forward, all I can say is, "I warned you!" I can assure you that our staff did not creatively fabricate these next two bosses. They do lurk somewhere out there in corporate America, making their employees retch on a daily basis. Now, if you have a weak stomach, you might want to skip ahead a page or so, because the two following letters are truly about "your worst nightmares!"

Gag Me Gussie

SHE'S MY WORST NIGHTMARE! At five foot two and weighing almost 275 pounds, she has long, dyed red frizzy hair that is greasy and matted. She talks with her mouth full of food and constantly interrupts others, but this is the nicest of her habits.

What irks me most is that, although suffering from a severe case of psoriasis on her hands, she has a compulsive habit of rubbing her hands together over her desk so the flakes fall off. Then she pokes the flakes into a pile with her index finger, licks her finger and picks up the flakes and eats them. Gag!!! If that's not bad enough, she scratches her head and eats the crud from under her fingernails. The pièce de résistance is when she picks her ears and gets a glob of earwax and then rolls it between her fingers and pops it into her mouth!

Many times she'll ask me if I'm mad or if something is on my mind because I'm looking down instead of at her. I'm afraid I'll throw up and sometimes have to leave her office because I am gagging. One thing for sure–I've learned not to arrange breakfast or luncheon meetings with her!

Your Worst Nightmare

OUR BOSS never lets you know when you are doing a good job, but the whole block knows when you make a mistake by his yelling. Recently, a customer called because he thought there was a mistake on his bill. The boss never looked up and just told the customer, "It must have been that time of the month for the girl who does the billing."

He always has his finger buried in his nose. After he
picks his nose, he wipes it on anything—like the walls, the
door frames, or even under the desk. Once when he took
me out to lunch, he picked his nose and wiped it on the
dinner plate. He spits repulsively on everything, and I
mean this man practically coughs up a lung when he spits.
He shocked a mechanic who was changing a tire when he
walked up and spit right on the tire the mechanic was
mounting on the car.

We've seen him taking his false teeth out and scraping
the crud off with a letter opener. This is matched only
when we see him taking his shoes and socks off so that he
can pick the toe jam out between his toes.

Finally, the ultimate stomach-turner is when he openly
urinates in a sewer about ten feet away from the bathroom
to save a few steps. He then will look around to see who's
watching him. Unbelievably, I've even seen him urinate on
truck tires.

For those of you who stayed with us and who felt your boss was
the worst of all, count your blessings. As I mentioned previously,
there just isn't anything that we can tastefully say about these
bosses. It truly boils down to a matter of self-esteem and respect
for others, or as we see above, the lack of it. We overlook and forgive many personality quirks in the people we work for, but there
is little excuse for these breaches in social etiquette and unhealthy
hygienic exhibitions. We can take comfort, however, that most
employees don't have to stomach such repulsive, nauseating spec-
tacles in their workplaces.

The descriptions of the following bosses buffer to some degree
the examples we just read. Do you see a contrast of respect and
deference for other people present in these bosses?

Our Agency Mood-Setter
DALE HAS CREATED a pleasant place to work and an
atmosphere much like that of a large family, where every
member has a different job to do yet each one helps the
other. We are treated respectfully like individuals, not just a
number. He is a thoughtful man of integrity, who truly cares

about other people's welfare. My definition of integrity is doing the right thing even though you could do the wrong thing and no one would ever know.

When our agency wins contests or meets goals, the administrative staff is always included with our spouses at parties and on trips. We went on a cruise to the Bahamas and a trip to Puerto Vallarta, and the crowning touch was when my boss sent me and my husband on our "dream trip," paying our airfare and hotel accommodations.

We all know that the agents sell to make our insurance agency profitable, but our boss has made the administrative staff feel that our jobs are just as important and that we make a valuable contribution to the agency. In fact he took us to the movies right in the middle of a workday to show his appreciation.

Innovative Board President

STEVE IS THE PRESIDENT of our Board of Trustees at our charity. The caring and creativity that Steve brings to our organization is not only a major element in our success, but also makes the job more fun and enjoyable.

His tireless energy and long hours are an inspiration to all of us, and his willingness to listen to opposing points of view and to try innovative and unconventional approaches to problem-solving make each day at work an exciting one.

Once a week, Steve buys lunch for the staff, giving us a feeling of family and an opportunity to exchange ideas and criticisms, and quite a few laughs. On Sundays during football season, Steve's house is turned into a virtual sports bar, with three televisions tracking the action via satellite hookup. Steve's wife puts on a gourmet feast for us and it's a great morale booster, but tough on our waistlines.

Good performances are rewarded with bonuses. He once paid for a staff trip to Las Vegas out of his own pocket after one stressful but successful program was completed. We had better luck with the program than with the gaming, but it was a great way for all of us to let off accumulated steam and it made us all feel appreciated.

Wouldn't we all like to work for and with a boss like Dale or Steve? Unquestionably, they have found the commonsense, simplistic answer to managing people successfully. They respect their people. They *treat their employees like family.*

What kind of impression do your customers, visitors, potential employees, not to mention your current staff, receive when they walk through the front door of your company? Do they feel special, respected, and appreciated? One of my favorite phrases is, "He's busier than a one-armed paperhanger with hives." We never should be too busy to create a pleasant environment in the workplace. Just as your grandmother's favorite cookie recipe calls for quality ingredients, the climate at work requires the best qualities in each of us—respect, integrity, consideration, understanding—to make the workplace enjoyable.

The Corporate Coach's Comments

Personal hygiene has always been an important issue in our country. Witness the huge emphasis on deodorants, perfumes, soaps—any and all personal care products—with which advertisers bombard the public. It's the sweet-smelling girl who gets her man and the fellow with the clean, wavy hair and smooth face who enchants the girl. But there are a number of countries around the world where cleanliness is *not* next to godliness. In many places, body odor is considered normal. Bathing is infrequent. Clothing is generally "aired out" rather than laundered.

The majority of the letters about gross bosses that we received, however, involved something other than cultural differences. They exposed bosses, as you read above, whose antics would turn anyone's stomach. It's hard to understand how and why people sink to such revolting behavior. But, as we discovered, the Gross Gusses are definitely present in all levels of corporate America and because of it, we must learn to deal with them. And dealing with them begins with trying to find a rationale for their conduct.

Thoughtless, disgusting slobs can emerge for several

reasons. There is the person who is so full of himself that he could not care less what people think. There also are those who may have such low self-esteem that they never look in the mirror and have no idea of, nor concern with, how they or their actions appear to others. A person who totally lets himself go hygienically can have a mental problem, needing professional help. But, perhaps the most difficult to tolerate is someone who performs these detestable deeds to shock others or to get his jollies.

Another person's personal hygiene is one of the most delicate and difficult subjects in the world to discuss. After all, it is a matter of comparison to your own, a matter of perspective, if you will. What is acceptable to you may not be normal, acceptable behavior to someone else. So, I see a couple of possible approaches to a boss afflicted with personally offensive hygiene habits.

If you should decide you can't tolerate the boss's offensive habits and you want to continue working for the company, gather your wits about you and approach him with a positive attitude. This is not a time to make accusations or judgments. Choose your words cautiously. Speak kindly and truthfully.

You might tell your boss you and your teammates are proud of your company and want to be especially proud of him. You can't beat around the bush; just tell your boss outright that you all believe his personal image needs polishing, which includes clean clothes, soap and water, and no more picking, flicking, or scratching. You will be taking a big gamble on this one, but some people get a new perspective when they see themselves as others see them, and actually clean up their acts.

If you don't want to confront the boss, you might try leaving my book on his desk, open to this chapter. You might try giving your boss a framed mirror frame for his desk so that he can be visually reminded of his disgusting habits. Seeing is believing! Or, if worst comes to worst, you may have to open the door to air out the office and just keep on walking—out of his office and out of the company.

Coach's Corner

TO THE EMPLOYEE:

☞ Make sure your own image is polished shiny clean before confronting anyone about personal habits. Don't risk a "pot calling the kettle black" reaction from coworkers.

☞ Approach your boss with concern about his habits without condemnation for the best reception possible.

☞ Apply the "golden rule" on a daily basis and treat others with the same respect you desire.

☞ Update your résumé and breathe the fresh air of opportunity, if you reach the end of your tolerance with your boss's hygienic deficiencies.

TO THE BOSS:

☞ Ponder how poor personal hygiene can affect morale and relationships with employees, as well as customers and others in your life.

☞ Show respect and consideration for your employees and notice the immediate progress you'll make in your working relationships.

☞ Fine-tune your personal habits and extend the same thoughtfulness and courtesy to family and associates. Watch all your relationships take a turn for the better.

CHAPTER 5

Corporate Controllers and Empowerment Experts

THINK FOR A MOMENT. Have you ever tried to push a piece of string in a straight line? If you do, you will quickly find out that the harder you push, the more it will coil and resist. On the other hand, what happens if you take that same piece of string and pull it? It will follow your fingers wherever they take it. Well, it works just the same on the job. Controlling bosses who use the *short leash* approach to management are constantly frustrated by employees who refuse to be pushed and prodded. In contrast, bosses who use the *long leash* technique or empowerment tend to find a whole lot of dedicated employees who will follow them to the ends of the earth.

The most common argument that I hear from bosses who follow the short-leash approach to management is that they believe they have to let the employees know who's the boss. Therefore, intimidation, humiliation, and fear are perfectly acceptable weapons to use to get the message across. What an unfortunate misunderstanding of management, not to mention human nature. Remember, the piece of string can be led, not pushed.

I should suggest one thing here. Employees should remember why bosses are bosses. It's generally because they have proven themselves to be competent people who someone higher up in the organization believes can help the company succeed. It is rarely the employee's job to tell the boss how to do his job. In other words, respect the role of the boss and remember that you were hired to do *your* job well, not the boss's.

Unfortunately, though, there are those bosses who haven't figured out that they don't have to beat their employees into submission to get the job done. These bosses go to some pretty unbelievable lengths to prove that they're in charge. Remember, there is a big difference between *"keeping your hand in the company"* and *"keeping your thumb on your employees."* Take for example the heavy-thumb approaches described in the excerpts below.

MY BOSS got his control jollies by personally scheduling our vacations, lunches, and reviews. If we got on his "bad side," he took responsibilities away and gave us degrading tasks with impossible goals, while openly criticizing us to our coworkers. The worst was when we saw our picture on his dartboard, as he drilled ten to twenty darts into our face.

~

OUR MANAGERS AND SUPERVISORS were invited to an elegant restaurant to celebrate the end of our company-wide program involving performance standards. A dining room full of patrons watched in horror at the restaurant's windows as our district manager let a squealing baby pig out of the backseat of his car. He demanded that, in our three-piece suits, we chase the pig across the lawn and remove a ribbon from the pig's neck that indicated we achieved the "scratch" or performance award. Our boss threatened those who refused to participate in this fiasco by saying, "Failure to chase the pig is a bad career choice!" Meanwhile, one patron actually called the animal cruelty society because the poor pig almost suffered a coronary.

~

MY BOSS MADE ME terminate employees once they reached a certain salary so he could hire someone new at a lesser wage. The clincher was when we were all asked to bark like a dog to receive our paychecks!

~

THE POSTAL PIRANHA who supervises my shift makes us ask permission to use the rest room and to get a drink of water. Talking is prohibited and sickness is absolutely unacceptable. Her expressed desire is to make life miserable for her "slaves" and to ridicule them into submissive obedience.

∾

OUR BOSS MAKES EMPLOYEES stand in front of his office window with hand raised, indicating that they need to use the bathroom. Worst of all, he stands on an elevated platform on Fridays after quitting time, waving paychecks. While employees stand at his feet, he asks, "Who will work mandatory overtime on Saturday?" His personal philosophy is, "If anyone disagrees with my decisions, fire them and string them up from the rafters!"

∾

HE CONTROLS with an iron fist! His edicts include, "No reading material allowed in the rest room even at lunch time or you lose your bonuses for the week...no walking on the grass...no discussing accounts with other departments...salespeople don't talk to credit people...full commission salespeople are required to punch a time clock...and I will choose your vacation week each year!"

∾

THE MONSTER I WORK FOR wanted to control the usage of the bathroom facilities so he put a padlock on the outside of the bathroom door. If you wanted to use it, you had to go find the security guard to unlock it and then you were allowed exactly two minutes. If you weren't out in two minutes, he would come in after you! He calls himself the "devil" and tries to intimidate and control everyone who crosses his path.

∾

MY BOSS SAT IN MY OFFICE, across my desk, using his laptop computer. He commonly answered my phone and opened my mail. He attended my meetings and seemed to take pleasure undermining my authority. If I crossed him, his wrath included slamming doors, throwing his laptop, or kicking the file cabinet. Instead of a manager, I felt like a puppet on a string, unable to make decisions on my own.

What on earth would allow a boss to believe that he was leading, motivating or in any other way *managing* a group of people if he finds it necessary to disgrace and dominate them at every turn? If that is the only way to get the job done, then there is a major problem. Making a successful salesman chase a pig to prove that he had achieved his performance level is absurd. It also makes me wonder what he made the salesmen do who *didn't* achieve their goals! Unfortunately, or fortunately, the letter didn't go into the sordid details of that fiasco! Similarly, making a worker who has earned a paycheck bark like a dog is ridiculous.

The problem with these bosses is that they lack the self-confidence and security to treat their employees with respect. They are afraid, for one reason or another, to leave their hands off and let their employees do their jobs. They think that the only way for them to stay on top and in control is to beat down those who report to them.

Managers deal shattering blows daily to employees' self-esteem with the short-leash management concept. It's like taking the dog for a walk and constantly pulling on the leash and yelling, "Heel!" That's the way a short-leash manager controls employees.

"Yes, but..." Isn't Empowerment

Many dominant bosses would be amazed at how intelligent and capable their employees are if given the opportunity to do their jobs. The fact of the matter is that one of the greatest keys to success is to let those who are best at the job do it without undue interference from the boss. Hire the best possible person to fill each position and get out of their way. Build their self-confidence by allowing them the right to do their jobs.

I've met countless company owners and CEOs over the years and seen this attitude firsthand. They "say" they empower employees and allow them to make decisions. When you ask them if they give employees total ownership of their jobs, the answer is usually, "*Yes, but...*" *Yes, but...*isn't empowerment.

I've also seen executives who paint a verbal picture of empowering employees with employee-suggestion programs. But when it comes time to "put their money and action where their mouth is," they maneuver evasively behind the lines like Roger "the dodger" Staubach did in his prime. These bosses are providing merely a glorified "*suggestion box*," not *empowerment* for their employees!

The contrast is obvious between the controllers described previously and the following bosses, who give more than mere lip service to the concept of empowerment. It doesn't take a magnifying glass to read between the lines of the excerpts below, in which employees describe bosses who show respect for their judgment by using the long-leash concept. These managers allow employees ownership of their jobs, as well as accountability for their decisions.

OUR SALES MANAGER, Mark, empowers each of us with the responsibility to manage our territories as our own small business. He allows us tremendous creativity in the critical decision-making process, yet is always there when we need guidance and direction. It's not uncommon to receive our weekly activity reports back via computer mail with ideas circled and positive comments and feedback inserted. He's extremely successful at fostering teamwork, loyalty, and dedication throughout our region.

∾

I'VE WORKED for my boss for twenty years, partly because he encourages us to investigate possibilities and come up with better ways of doing things. He allows us to be flexible and experiment with our ideas. For example, we are now open to patrons on Wednesday evenings and flex our workload accordingly. He teaches others skills so they can be better at what they do. For example, he leads summer workshops in media production for teachers who want to make their own media materials.

∾

IT'S NOT UNUSUAL to see my petite dynamo boss in sneakers, dressed in a football uniform, presenting her

ideas about effective teamwork to our top management.
Lynn is young and energetic, and she's determined to
empower her employees. When she was asked to present
the workings of our department to the corporate CEO, she
saw a chance for her employees to shine and demonstrate
our knowledge and expertise. She let us develop the material, create visuals, and deliver the actual presentation.
Thanks to her, the CEO knows now who we are and what
we do. She let us "shine."

∾

MY BOSS has hired educated, experienced people whom he
encourages to aim even higher. He allowed me the independence to build programs and establish procedures in
our agency. "I have to listen to people's ideas," I once over-
heard him say, "because their ideas are good." Even though
he initially opposed one of my projects, he supported it
with his own suggestions, and the plan produced results in
spite of his reservations. He took none of the credit, but
instead recommended me for a quality step increase.

∾

MELANIE WEARS MANY HATS including doctor, employer,
administrator, and friend. She educates and empowers her
employees. She "opens windows of the mind that were
heretofore closed, enabling growth professionally and personally." What more could I ask for my role model?

∾

WHEN WE MOVED our office into her new home, she asked
my opinion on decisions about our new office furniture,
drapes, decorative accessories, and even storage requirements.
She said, "Pick whatever you want." She told me to select
seven pieces from our decorative accessory business that I
would like to have in our office and she got them for me.

∾

MY BOSS ALWAYS looked for the good in people and
believed that everyone could do the jobs assigned. When I
worked for him, I was going to night school to finish my

degree in hopes of getting a promotion. He helped me reach my goal by giving me assignments that were outside my normal job descriptions. He treated me like the rest of his staff and never limited what I was given to do. He made all his employees stretch and reach to do projects. He was confident enough to leave us alone to do what was assigned, even though he was always available to give us a hand.

It's impossible for any manager to be everywhere at all times, so employees must be trusted to represent the company to customers. And if you go to the trouble of screening and hiring the best employees you can find, let them think and act in your behalf. Any coach will tell you, "a team will outperform a group of individuals any time." My business philosophy always has been to hire the best people I could find—*people who are smarter than me*. Train them, coach them, empower them, tell them what you expect from them and then get out of their way, and let them push the company *and their boss* to the top.

Changing Management Mind-Set

Several years ago, I received a desk plaque from Chuck Harstad, division vice president of 3M Commercial Office Supply Division, which I would like to share with you. It epitomizes what we're talking about.

The Changing Management Mind-Set

From:	*To:*
Managing Others	Leading Others
Directing	Guiding
Competing	Collaborating
Relying on Rules	Focusing on Outcomes
Using Hierarchy	Using Network
Consistency/Sameness	Diversity/Flexibility
Secrecy	Sharing Information
Passivity	Risk Taking
Isolation	Involvement
People as an Expense	People as an Asset

One of the best teaching aids is reading comparison situations. In the following letters, employees contrast bosses who control and those who empower. We must empathize with the first two and definitely applaud the second two.

The Master of Mind Games

OUR BOSS IS A MASTER at playing mind games, but when employees learn the ground rules and how to play his games, he changes the rules. He told our department managers, "A good supervisor constantly keeps his subordinates *off balance.*"

He hired good people, but became paranoid when they displayed any intelligence. In ten years he hired and eliminated ten administrators with his "sick games." He would give them lengthy assignments and when they were completed, he would scream at the administrator for wasting time on something he had not approved. With nothing in writing, the subordinate had no proof!

He loved to promote new people quickly, and as soon as they bought a house and felt secure, he immediately demoted them for incompetence.

After encouraging one woman to decorate her office with plants, he told her to get rid of them immediately. She took several home that night, but was put on permanent probation the following Monday because all the plants weren't removed.

His sadistic trait surfaced often, but the worst was when he disliked a crippled woman who parked in the lot behind the building next to ours. If he arrived first, he'd lock the back door so that she would have to limp on ice and snow around the building to the front door.

One secretary was ten minutes late two consecutive days during a heavy snowstorm. He yelled the first day and ordered her into his office the second day. Rather than face him again, she resigned immediately. He then fired her for insubordination and bragged how her employee record would be tarnished.

He gave another employee notice on her wedding anniversary, right after she received flowers from her husband.

The Tongue of A Viper, Dripping with Venom

SHE HAS THE TONGUE OF A VIPER, dripping with venom, and she's the worst control freak ever. She approves days off for vacation and then makes us cancel our vacation and work instead–after all the plans and reservations are made. She changes our days off to suit her moods. If a holiday lands on a weekend, we don't get the day off. Routinely, she makes employees work through lunch and then doesn't let them take their lunch. No Christmas decorations are allowed, and she doesn't send Christmas cards to customers, much less buy gifts for anyone. Benefits are a joke!

She ridicules and screams at employees in front of coworkers and visitors. She calls us into meetings, points out any and all mistakes in front of anyone who happens to be attending the meeting. She uses filthy language to and around employees and tells people they're stupid. Her temper tantrums include throwing things, slamming doors, and pouting.

She has no integrity, manners, or managerial skills, and cannot hold a discussion without being rude and sarcastic. One of her favorite pastimes is turning employees against one another as she lies to everyone, telling them their coworkers don't like them. She overloads people with work, then sets impossible deadlines. If you tell her you worked overtime, instead of being grateful, she tells you it was because you couldn't get your work done. She says, "People who can't get their work done can be fired!"

It's routine for her to threaten our jobs. She loves to fire people on Christmas Eve! Her best trick is to wait until employees are due raises, and then she fires them. In fact, she draws childish pictures of the people she fires, tapes the pictures to their empty chair, and makes fun of the "departed" employee. There's a file documenting every employee's mistakes in her desk drawer. Our boss even makes us crawl on the rug all over the office and under our desk to pick up staples out of the carpet.

Some bosses, like those above, still haven't grasped the concept that you get more from employees if you lead them instead of push them. Remember the string example? Compare the differences in philosophy of the bosses below.

Executive "Sweet" Boss

I RESPONDED TO AN AD for *someone with a brain to administer the needs of a medium-sized office suite* and found the "sweetest" best boss ever.

He started my first day with a gift-wrapped box of personalized business cards and gave me an important "title" to let clients know I was as important to the company as he. He also took me to all his business meetings and introduced me to his associates.

He gave me full power to totally furnish his "start-up" office, and gave me my choice of offices. He also allows me to use the computer outside of work to make extra money.

My boss gives me full decision-making power over my domain and backs me up with clients when disagreements arise. He listens to my occasional gripes or joys that I care to share and doesn't burden me too much with his own gripes, yet shares all his joys.

This true gentleman never, never puts me in a precarious or questionable situation and always is complimentary and shows his gratitude with a sincere "*thank you.*"

Empowerment Educator

FOR TWO YEARS my manager gave me the single most important quality that a manager can give his or her employee—self-esteem. He did this by displaying a number of leadership dimensions and acting as a role model for me and others in our company.

He really knew what "empowerment" meant. He considered me valuable—valuable enough to influence his management decisions. *He provided me with an environment where my input was respected.*

How did I become so empowered and gain self-esteem? I learned daily in his empowerment tutelage. My boss taught me to be a leader. He trained me how to influence others by communicating persuasively and by using inventive forms of daily communication, such as electronic mail, telephone, conference calls, select meetings, etc.

He tutored me to manage my projects and to build and manage teams. He recognized the importance of managing diverse work groups (i.e., women, people of all races and nationalities) and that is why he asked me to be involved in a number of diversity programs including INROADS (a minority students' summer internship program).

Finally, and most importantly, he taught me to care for people. Many times he would call my wife for permission to keep me at the office for some overtime work. He always would remember to send her a thank you for her sacrifice and contribution to my career.

These bosses have figured it out. They have bought into the concepts that motivation, kindness, and leadership beat that of harassment and intimidation.

I'm reminded of an interview I did recently with a magazine writer. When he asked me how I would define success today in the business world, I responded without hesitation. I told him, "To me, success is when I can walk through our buildings and look at employees whose self-esteem, confidence, and independence have improved because of the empowerment environment that we've created." That's success!

The Corporate Coach's Comments

The business world will never rid itself of bosses who believe that they must control and dominate in order to get the job done. It's just too much a part of the thinking of many long-established bosses. But maybe these bosses can understand that their jobs can be easier and their people more productive if they empower and coach their employees. After all, both bosses and their employees are just trying to do their jobs and get ahead. Communication, understanding, and just a little old-fashioned kindness may be all it takes to turn an uncommitted employee into a company man and a dictator boss into a productive manager.

A vast majority of the bosses are good people who are trying to manage their employees in the best way they know how. Unfortunately, even many of these well-intentioned bosses forget that their job isn't to do the work, but to see to it that the work gets done. Bosses who take too much of a hands-on approach need to be reminded that an employee is most useful if he is allowed to do his job.

So how do you tell a boss to leave you alone and let you do the job you were hired to do? The first step is to try to understand *why* the boss is behaving the way he is. There are usually two possibilities.

On the one hand, the problem may be with the boss. Check to see how he treats the rest of the folks who report to him. Chances are that if he meddles in everyone's work, the problem lies with him. He may be incapable of "letting go." This is a tough one, because the problem is deeply rooted in his inability to trust other people. If this is what you're dealing with, the chances of changing his behavior are pretty slim. However, even in these instances, it may be possible to make some improvement. Try this approach.

Tell the boss that you appreciate that he's deeply concerned with the quality of the work you're performing, and you would like to *earn* the right to put his mind at ease and prove that you can handle it. Suggest that he make you a trade. He'll give you more room and you'll agree to a system of cross-checks that will keep him apprised of your actions. For example, suggest that initially, you and he schedule a standing meeting every morning at 9:00. At these meetings you can discuss progress and plans. Tell him that you would understand that at the beginning these meetings should be frequent and detailed. Then work out a timetable over which, with good performance, the meetings would become less frequent and rigorous. The boss will get his security and you'll get a chance to wean him away.

The second situation in which bosses won't let go is when the problem is with the employee. Most often this happens where a boss simply can't trust the employee to do his job well. If you check around and find that the boss is hands-off with most of the employees but has you under his thumb, look honestly at your performance. Set up an appointment and ask the boss point-blank whether you're making the grade with your work. Once you've asked, he can tell you one of two things.

If he tells you that you're not performing up to standards, you can immediately grasp the opportunity to ask for more guidance. He may even give you credit for perceiving that a problem exists. Many times this kind of communication will allow corrections to be made before the boss loses patience and deals with your poor performance through drastic measures.

If the boss says that you're doing a great job, then you are in a perfect position to ask him for more elbow room. After all, he's just admitted that you can do the job. He may be blind to the fact that you're ready to take it on your own, and your questions will wake him up.

Regardless, you need to find out what's going on if you're not being permitted to do your job. You may or may not like what you learn, but at least you'll know where you stand— and you can make your decisions from there.

Coach's Corner

TO THE EMPLOYEE:

☛ Try to understand why your boss is determined to control. Is it your performance or his insecurity?

☛ Evaluate whether the boss is overly controlling of only your work, or everyone's.

☛ Give your honest, constructive opinions when asked for input.

☛ Remember who's the boss and keep your dignity.

☛ Do your job well and allow the boss to give you the elbow room you desire.

TO THE BOSS:

☛ Treat employees with dignity and respect. It's in your own economic interest to do so.

☛ Remember that you're the boss. Your time can be better spent managing rather than doing others' work.

☛ Listen to employees and ask for input. They are often closer to the problems and their solutions may be better than yours.

☛ Remember it's easier to pull a string than to push one.

CHAPTER 6

Superstars and Coaches

He strutted around the office like a peacock and proclaimed, "He's the man!" He ranted and raved that employees didn't do anything right. His idea of motivation was calling everyone stupid losers.

SOUND FAMILIAR? It's no wonder that this boss was nominated as a worst boss and that his employees struggle in a constant state of stress. There are bosses around the world who are convinced that "It's my way or the highway." The idea of teamwork is absolutely foreign to them. Whether the cause is a lack of confidence or trust in employees, a compulsion to stand out as the ultimate authority, or an ego that needs continual stroking, the effect remains the same: a boss whose idea of teamwork is "I'll do it myself" or "You do it; I don't have time" rather than "Let's do it together as a team." These drillmasters are joined by others, who surfaced in our worst boss contest, suffering from the same delusion.

THIS MONSTER SHOWED HIS FACE in the office about one hour a day, but in that time, he created animosity between staff members by threatening to replace one person with another. He gave the same assignment to multiple people and claimed it was the only way he could get things done.

~

I BELIEVE she was an honor graduate of "The Attila the Hun School of Management!" Her idea of teamwork was when I took projects from beginning almost to completion,

then she would take the final product and all files from my
office when I was gone. She would present the project as
her own and take all the credit. The board was told that I
had done nothing to help!

~

NEVER MIND that she yelled at us on a daily basis or treated
us like children. As she laughed in your face, any suggestions
given to her were ridiculed, only to surface a couple months
later as her ideas to be incorporated into the business routine.
She would take aside one person at a time and poison that
person's mind against the other people in the office, saying
that other employees didn't like that person. We weren't
allowed to socialize with other staff members during or after
work. If we got too friendly, she'd find a way to drive a
wedge between us.

~

MY BOSS is a consummate suck-up artist who sacrifices
staff morale and democratic standards merely to look good.
He also has a unique management style that I call "the
shotgun method." Whenever a situation arises that requires
a conscious well-aimed team decision, he instead will
bypass the hows and whys and blast both barrels into his
own conclusions. This results in a decision that makes no
sense to anyone, is completely unfair, and proves that
"there is an I in the word TEAM."

~

SHE ALWAYS WAS PRESENT to take credit when our
department received any kind of praise or acclaim. Yet if I
needed advice, she would say, "That's your job, don't
expect me to help." Not solving problems to her satisfaction, though, would result in the usual tirade and screaming
insults that always ended with, "If you don't like it, don't
let the door hit your butt on the way out!"

~

MY WORK CREATED too much publicity for the Ice
Queen. Articles about our work and company never men-

tioned my contributions to our success. My boss said, "This is for your benefit, so you won't have to turn down job offers!" I made six dollars an hour and drove a 1964 Plymouth at the time, and my image-conscious queen made me park in the alley so I would not risk my professional image. On icy days, however, I was to leave home early to be on time to work. My boss lived half a mile from the office and needed a ride. Her reason was: "This is the difference between an old Plymouth and a new BMW—we do not risk the latter."

While the creation of trust is an ongoing process that doesn't happen overnight, the bosses mentioned in the letters above probably will always perceive their employees as inadequate and worthy of suspicion. They appear to have no confidence in their people, to the point of performing the habitual "lone ranger" routine. Unfortunately, this approach never works. No company exists where one person can do it all. From answering the phones to emptying trash to selling products to hiring new employees, the number of tasks to be done in a successful business is staggering. While it's possible to develop good teammates, the easiest way to build a great team is to hire winners and achievers. At our companies, we spend a lot of time, energy, and effort on making sure that we hire good people. We don't do it for fun—we do it because experience has proven time and time again that good people make good companies. People are the foundation and, just as in the foundation of a building, all the pieces must fit together and support one another to get the job done. There is no room for the guy who tries to go it alone.

In fact, we give our managers a plaque with this philosophy spelled out for a constant reminder:

A Short Course in HUMAN RELATIONS

The six most important words:
I admit I made a mistake.
The five most important words:
You did a good job!

The four most important words:
What is your opinion?

The three most important words:
If you please.

The two most important words:
Thank you.

The single most important word:
We

The least important word:
I

Working Together (as a TEAM) is Success!

It's also important to remember that your folks are different. From time to time, experienced managers restructure their teams. They shuffle the players so that star performers can learn from other stars. And they realize that the "also-rans" can benefit from watching how different stars do it. Competition and cooperation—that's what it's all about. Competition stimulates action, cooperation cements the team spirit, and *teamwork* is the result.

Teamwork can be and should be employed in every area of the company. For example, quality involvement teams within departments will alert management to problem areas and, nearly always, will offer experienced suggestions to correct those problems. Structured sales teams create a competitive atmosphere that naturally will increase the company's sales efforts. Customer service teams provide customers the assurance of knowing exactly who will handle any need that arises. Clerical and administrative teams can support and cross train one another in numerous responsibilities. Stockers and shippers in the warehouse can form teams to increase productivity and to observe one another's safety procedures. The opportunities for profiting through teamwork truly are limitless. And, like concentric circles, the perimeters will grow continuously.

When you have your team functioning well on all eight cylinders, consider the ripple effect by including your suppliers, vendors, and customers. *When we're all in it together*, the tasks become easier, are handled more professionally, and are a lot more fun!

The bosses portrayed in the letters below have come to the same conclusions. It's understandable why their employees consider them among the best.

MIKE ISN'T A BOSS AT ALL–he's our coach! He says, "It takes everyone doing their part to create our team." Managing by walking around, he continually reassures us that "We're all in this together." He infuses our meetings with brain games which stimulate creative flow, contribute to team cooperation, and uphold mental alertness. Instead of using impersonal formalities such as "staff," his memos are addressed to "teammates or friends."

∽

DOUG IS A "SEEDER." He plants ideas and knowledge, helps them to grow, and allows his employees to reap the rewards. He builds his teams knowing that the individual's contribution strengthens the whole and every "shining star" gets to have their day. He is a "shielder" because personal attacks are never allowed in his departments. He provides for open forum, brainstorming, fair play, opportunity, and growth. Most importantly, he allows for the "humanness" in each of us, never losing sight of the whole picture.

∽

LEE ADMINISTERS personality/behavior profiles periodically so we might all understand and continue to understand each other, even as we grow and change through the years. She promotes growth and self-esteem and encourages constructive criticism even if it might be unfavorable to her personally; then works to correct and/or construct new directions. She promotes staff development by encouraging us to attend and travel to any training opportunities applicable to our position, e.g., cooking workshops, financial seminars, abuse workshops, stress reduction workshops, working with difficult people seminars, and education workshops. She constantly strives to upgrade our equipment and facilities and cares about our health, wellness, and working environment.

∾

IN 1989, our department was "frozen in place" to undergo reorganization every six to eight weeks. While I watched other managers transfer out of this chaos as soon as they could, leaving their people demoralized, angry, and frightened, never once did I hear Burt telling anyone to stop complaining and leave him alone because he wasn't responsible for what was happening to us. When he heard, even secondhand, that someone in the department was depressed or upset, he would make a point of dropping in on that person to talk the problem through. We felt that Burt really cared about us and our careers. He was willing to fight for us whether it was in setting up a development plan, job interviews, or getting recognition from the organization. Even hardened cynics such as myself came to trust his word because he put himself and his own career on the line, showing that he was not just spouting rhetoric.

∾

LARRY'S NOT A DESK JOCKEY. He gets out and gets involved. Whether it's out in the field working side by side with the service techs or sales inspectors, or answering phones and working in the office, he works as part of our team—not just the leader.

∾

BEFORE JAMES CAME ABOARD, we were failing miserably at our jobs, but had no idea we were. Then he entered our lives and within days, he showed us the hows and whys by doing it himself. We learned from a true leader. Attitudes were positive, goals were set, budgets were hit, and the company officers noticed us. James gave us, his team, all the credit.

∾

BARBARA IS EXCELLENT at encouraging teamwork, real teamwork, where members work towards a common goal of increased productivity and sustained higher level of quality.

She encourages social team activities, such as bowling tour-
naments, chili cook-offs, and departmental potluck lun-
cheons. If an employee is a little slower to complete an
assignment or needs a little more direction than others, as
our true coach, Barbara will encourage the person to keep
him from getting discouraged, so that he can feel the satisfaction of completing the job.

Show me a successful company with a highly motivated workforce, and I'll show you a management dedicated to a coaching
philosophy of teamwork and employee involvement. A job worth
doing is worth doing together, because teamwork divides the task
and doubles the success! Obviously, this same game plan is practiced by the coaches above because their team has voted them
Best Bosses—and rightly so.

In the second half, however, we see a quarterback sneak on the
part of the following bosses who make a mockery of teamwork.

A 1920s Sweatshop

IN THE ELEVEN YEARS that I have worked for my
boss, I have yet to hear a single word of praise or
encouragement. Yet for twenty years, my previous
employers praised my work in glowing terms, and I was
given regular merit increases. His management philosophy
doesn't allow for words of praise. In fact, his theory is that
browbeating and verbal whippings are the way to get
things done.

My boss never has assigned me to a single objective or
goal that was attainable, preferring to put me in a position
where my failures will be inevitable. And when it comes
annual review time, he reminds me of underachievements
when doling out meager increases.

He's impossible to talk to and constantly discounts
any idea for improvement that anyone suggests. We
expect a conversation with him to be liberally spiced
with four-letter words, verbal put-downs, and in the right
environment, clouds of cigar smoke. He has personally
ruined the interiors of over a hundred rental cars and
motel rooms with his burning stench.

The longer I work for this man, whose management style is right out of a 1920s sweatshop, the less value I have to any other company. He has taken away my professional edge and replaced it with dulled acceptance of unfulfilled goals. I will never forgive him.

The Legal Eagle Soars Alone

OUR BARRISTER would sell his soul, if he had one, for career advancement. He has two rules: "He does whatever he wants...and...everyone else does whatever he wants." He controls all communication avenues. We may not initiate direct conversations with management or take credit for anything. He claims all the honors and accepts none of the blame when things go wrong. He demands copies of all E-mail, and all oral discussions must be summarized in E-mail to him. This removes any avenue of grievance.

He treats professional staff like clerical staff, and clerical staff like serfs. Nobody may question his authority, offer opinions, or propose anything independently. Your only chance of implementing an idea is to convince him it's his. His moods change instantaneously, from childish to abusive. If employees don't play along, they are evaluated as emotional and resistant to leadership–his!

Although he is rarely in the office, we're told to say he's always available to assist. The problem is only vice presidents and above may speak with him directly, and he's only interested in people who can do things for him.

These two bosses shoved teamwork and empowerment to the edge, plunging them full speed into the credibility gap. How often do we hear friends or family members complain about a boss who is a glory hound, always craving all the credit and fame and wanting none of the hassle or work involved to complete a project? This situation is so evident in the first two essays. These bosses haven't yet discovered the secret of unleashing their employees' creative juices in order to profit through their knowledge and ingenuity. When they do–like the next two bosses–they will unearth the cornerstone necessary to building a company based on teamwork.

Show me bosses like those below, who create a supportive, not threatening, atmosphere, and I'll show you a successful company where mistakes are treated as opportunities for growth and learning. In the final analysis, either we're pulling together or we're pulling apart. The next two bosses certainly practice this management philosophy.

An Ode to A Coach

Please take a moment to read about my boss
He's the best among the best...he'll always win the toss!
It takes a special person to be in top command,
Leading people to the task, without a forceful hand.
In all he does and all he says, he's consistent, fair and kind,
Providing special care and guidance with the individual in mind.
Building, growing, training, teaching...these things he does best,
Urging us to know our strengths, and putting them to the test.
Reaching for the top is what we're taught to do,
Guiding with his wisdom, he's right beside us too.
Empowering all his leaders, as success takes more than one,
Standing near to coach and cheer, until the job is done.

The Coach Showcases His Team's Talent

BOB IS A CORPORATE BOSS who provides opportunities for the nontraditional worker, he passes on the "cookie cutter" applicant and hires the unconventional, yet qualified candidate. Our monthly meetings are filled with encouraging words. Not only does he give credit when credit is due, he has helped me utilize my time to develop the skills I need to become a marketable commodity in the corporate environment.

He encouraged me to set up a meeting with the new vice president to explain a marketing plan I had developed for a project I was working on. Most bosses would have stolen the idea and the credit, but Bob is proud of my talent and ideas and wanted me to showcase them before upper management. He's never threatened when I develop a concept that is in opposition to his own; his ego is never involved in his work.

Bob's pet project at work is a nonprofit charity organization called Peas on Earth, which raises money for needy families and distributes it during the holidays. Peas on

Earth was set up by Bob, who raises money by putting together and selling an employee cookbook. When I composed a letter asking employees to donate recipes to his pet project, he asked me if I minded adding his name under mine on the letterhead. Another boss simply would have put his name on the letter and deleted mine.

Bob's true colors came shining through last week, when I was offered a temporary position by the Marketing Department. Bob's department is already short-staffed and he's losing two key people in the summer. The decision to let me go was his alone, and he gave me his blessing, saying it was too good a career move for me to pass up.

Whether in prose or poetry, these bosses captured the essence of coaching and mentoring to employees. The background information in "An Ode to A Coach" indicated that, as a college professor and mentor for years, this boss entered the business world stressing the importance of the individual with a philosophy that "people are our greatest resource." I couldn't agree more!

The Corporate Coach's Comments

I have known some truly outstanding bosses over the years—great *superstars*—who are delightful, humble people, who wouldn't dream of strutting their stuff at the expense of others. Successful bosses, however, sometimes possess a well-developed ego. Actually, that's one of the assets that make them good at what they do. However, when that ego begins to become more important than the team, there is trouble brewing. To be most effective, a boss must fulfill his ego through the success of his *team* and realize that if the team is not successful, he is not successful.

Let me suggest, however, that it may not be wrong for the boss to be the one in the spotlight. After all, success and failure are his responsibility. In a team effort it's not who gets the accolades that matters but rather the fact that the job gets done and done well. We sometimes get hung up on who gets credit rather than the end result. As long as everyone contributes to the overall effort and as long as the boss appreciates and knows that your role was essential, kudos are secondary in importance.

The bottom line is this: When it comes to credit, sometimes the world is unfair. Keep in mind, however, that in the long run the cream will rise to the top and you may well find yourself moving past your ego-driven boss on the ladder of success!

Coach's Corner

TO THE EMPLOYEE:

☞ Be willing to sacrifice individual goals for team goals to have a great team.

☞ Don't let an ego-driven boss destroy your personal sense of achievement.

☞ Remember that bosses not only get all the credit, they also generally get all the blame.

☞ Teamwork divides the task and doubles the success.

TO THE BOSS:

☞ Remember to appreciate all employees and their contributions when you find yourself in the spotlight.

☞ Recognize employees' accomplishments with praise and rewards.

☞ Consider the positive effects that structuring teams throughout your company will have on employees.

☞ Evaluate the people chemistry and the personality traits for the best harmony possible as you form your teams.

☞ Let your employees take the credit for their triumphs and successes. You will be amazed how their self-esteem and productivity will improve.

CHAPTER 7

Hypocrites and WYSIWYGs

(What you see is what you get)

WHAT HE SAYS: *"I want my people to take the initiative in their work areas."*
WHAT HE MEANS: *"If they try to undermine my authority, I'll yell and ridicule them publicly."*

WHAT HE SAYS: *"I can't afford Christmas bonuses or profit sharing this year. It's been a lean year for the company."*
WHAT HE MEANS: *"I need the extra income for my new Mercedes, my son's tuition at Yale, and the trip to Europe that I promised my wife."*

WHAT HE SAYS: *"I have to let you go. The company's downsizing is necessary because we just aren't making enough money to make payroll."*
WHAT HE MEANS: *"The rest of the employees can carry the load while I supervise the ten-thousand-dollar redecorating project of my office."*

Get the picture? With a hypocrite, "what you see" definitely isn't "what you get!" A letter I received recently described this situation perfectly.

THE BOUQUET OF BALLOONS on my desk were a rainbow of colors and each had words of praise. "Congratulations!" "Good Luck!" What a nice touch from my boss after I landed the major account our company had romanced for months! I knew my boss was ecstatic when I left for the weekend, and I was on cloud nine. As I opened the card, I was confused by his message, "Good luck on your new job." What new job? My boss stepped out of his office and said, "The job you are going to look for today. YOU'RE FIRED! I decided two months ago to cut overhead and let you go, but waited until our big account was secure."

Can you believe this guy? I often wonder what makes people like this tick. Why go to all the trouble of the balloons and all that if the goal was to fire the person? This is premeditated nastiness and a sure sign of a two-faced, good-for-nothing hypocrite!

Hypocrisy is really just a hybrid type of dishonesty. It makes you believe one thing when another is true. I think that it may be a little less evil than garden-variety dishonesty because hypocrites often don't realize their own behavior. But it's still wrong.

In these situations, the person is manipulating others through his behavior, not just reflecting the changes from day-to-day life. In our company we believe in the concept of *transparency*. What we mean is that a person should be simple and straightforward in his dealings with others. No masks, no games, no roles. What you see is what you get.

Life is so much simpler when the game playing is eliminated from the relationship. It really does work best this way. When there is a problem or an issue that needs to be discussed, invite the employee in for a talk. In the meeting, talk honestly and directly about the issues at hand. Whatever is discussed should be treated professionally and used to improve the team. The discussion should be confidential and not leave the room. You'd be amazed at the results when issues are addressed head-on rather than in the cloak-and-dagger manner that hypocrites use!

We've all encountered hypocrites in our lives. Some justify their "shading the truth" by saying that they're just trying to make everyone happy, to make things run smoothly. Others delude themselves that they are doing what's necessary to get the work done.

Both of these types of hypocrites may be well intentioned, but they nevertheless tend to confuse issues and mislead others. Even though they are trying hard to help, in the long run they'll probably cause hurt feelings, miscommunications, and trouble. They would be much farther ahead to hit it "head on" and do their jobs in a more straightforward manner.

The ones who affect us most are the bosses who purposely mislead others, knowing full well that they're setting them up for a fall. You never can be sure that there's not another double-cross lurking around the corner.

Now, let's get to the excerpts from the following letters for some eye-opening accounts of almost unbelievable hypocrisy. Whatever the reasons that these bosses have decided that the end justifies the means, they are certainly off track. It doesn't take a crystal ball to identify the problems present in each of these bosses.

WHAT A PHONY! Our boss yelled at an employee for incompetence, inefficiency, and violation of policy. The next morning, Secretary's Day, he left a card on her computer, thanking her for her hard work and invaluable contribution! He enforced a five-day suspension without pay against one employee beginning December 5, then sent an invitation to join him "for wine and cheese after work" on December 8. He hired an instructor as a consultant, then arbitrarily fired him, depriving him of $20,000. Then he sent the dismissed employee a birthday card, urging him to have a wonderful day!

∼

MY BOSS'S INCONSISTENCIES can be so frustrating. For example, less than a month after circulating a memo pertaining to the misuse of computer resources—especially playing games—and when I was facing an imminent and very critical deadline, he took five hours out of my day to have me install a new computer game on his machine!

∼

HE WAS VERY OVERWEIGHT and wore a wig. With summer temperatures over one hundred degrees, he would wear short shorts and T-shirts, while we were required to wear nylons and dresses. He gave a fifteen-cent raise once a year, but stopped this extravagance when he decided to build a new office next door. The whole top floor of the building consisted of his personal kitchen, full bath, pool table, meeting and sitting rooms. His desk alone was a monstrous curved mahogany masterpiece. Yet, we continued to work in cramped cubicles in the adjacent building—just making him money.

∾

MY BOSS WON'T DEVELOP his employees or permit them to do any work that is managerial. He does make an exception if a project is going to be late due to his mismanagement. He then assigns the project to an employee and blames the employee for the problem. When rumors about a merger made employees uneasy last year, our boss held a meeting to affirm that our company had no plans to eliminate our jobs. Last month, when the announcement was made that our jobs are ending because of the joint venture, my boss bragged how hard he worked on this project for more than fourteen months.

∾

THE DAY BEFORE THANKSGIVING, our boss amended holiday pay for new employees which caused them to lose four paid holidays, yet his pay wasn't affected by the holiday. He said he couldn't give anyone a raise or supply needed tools because of company financial trouble, yet company funds paid for his Mercedes, and his costly tropical fish arrived daily at the shop. He even commented, "I might have to sell this Mercedes, or my BMW, or one of my other two cars just to keep things going."

∾

THE LAW PARTNERSHIP had a very good year and then, after taking their year-end bonus, they put the staff on a four-day work week with a 20 percent pay cut. If this wasn't bad enough, my boss, Mr. Sensitive, said that if this caused me any problems, I should bring in my bills and he would help me with my budget (implying that I couldn't manage my money). In the fall the senior partner traded his company car for a new Volvo and drove it for two months. He traded it for a new Jeep for the winter season and then traded it in for a Mercedes. A new Porsche (another company car) replaced the Mercedes in a couple of months. Now, the car business is really none of my concern; however, we were just put on a four-day work week again, with a 20 percent cut in pay. He added "Now, I don't want any attitudes around here!"

~

OURS IS A CORPORATION of cold-blooded sharks and my boss is the "great white" in the lead. She routinely speaks negatively of superiors behind their backs and then is their biggest cheerleader to their faces. She reads her employees "the riot act," and denies it to superiors when confronted about an incident. She preaches the team credo, then states, "They are just my workers, my people, doing my methods of work."

Keeping employees constantly off guard with these hocus-pocus antics is a guaranteed way to undermine morale and create dissension at work. Let's face it. The atmosphere of a workplace is either positive or negative. And you never have a positive climate when a boss believes, "Do as I say, not as I do." He may not verbalize this belief, but his actions consistently (or rather inconsistently) will speak louder than his words.

Being True To One's Colors

The inconsistent behavior, the unkept promises, the hypocrisy in dealing with others–it all gets back to a question of honesty. It's more than a matter of outright lying to people. It's more than trying to cheat people for personal gain. And, rest assured, we'll deal with liars and cheats in a subsequent chapter in this book. But, I'm talking here about saying one thing to people while, in your heart, you have a different agenda in mind all along. I'm talking about underhanded planning and scheming as opposed to an "off the cuff" remark. And having to cope with anyone who isn't true to his colors is frustrating and demoralizing–particularly if that person is your boss.

When employees feel they have been treated fairly and honestly, the mirror image returns. They, in turn, treat others fairly and honestly. That would include bosses, coworkers, and customers. It's the ripple effect.

Effective, successful managers realize that if you want your employees to treat customers and clients well, you have to treat your employees well. It's that simple. Employees who feel mistreated at work are not going to go "the extra mile" for the customer, and without a loyal customer base, the company's growth and survival are almost impossible.

But let's see how the truly successful managers approach this topic. What a contrast we see in the following excerpts that show-case bosses who have made integrity their lifestyle.

MY BOSS BLENDS BUSINESS STRATEGIES, kindness, generosity, and caring for his employees. He doesn't boast about his deeds and is humble enough to admit when he makes a mistake. He gives and expects quality work and professionalism in the office and encourages fun at appropriate times.

~

I'VE WORKED "with," not "for," Craig for ten years because that's the kind of atmosphere he generates. He treats people up and down the corporate ladder equally, without regard to titles or hierarchies implied in the real world. I've seen him stop board meetings to greet dietary workers on our staff just as quickly as he does to greet hospital benefactors.

~

THE PERFECT BOSS may not exist, but I do believe that my boss, Peter, is truly an ideal boss. He provides his employees with rich Colombian coffee and real half-and-half cream. Yet, he gets his own coffee throughout the day. One of our best medical technicians underwent brain surgery and was left with physical impairments that made it impossible for her to perform many of her duties. Rather than place her on disability retirement (as the insurance policy provides), Peter simply amended her duties and maintained her on staff, where she is still a valued employee.

~

BILL WAS A SENIOR VICE PRESIDENT at our bank for years. His approach toward life and work was to create an atmosphere of trust where everyone worked toward the same goals. He trusted those who reported to him to meet standards of excellence—yet he expected no less of us than he did of himself. Although he hated bad weather, he often drove twelve miles or so out of his way to pick up employees who were apprehensive about driving on ice.

～

An Ode to Edward

He's a man of his word, a quality rare,
When a job's to be done, you will find him there.
No stuffed-shirt executive; places all his own calls;
No frivolous accolades paper his walls.
His life's like a sermon; without him preaching,
His words and actions reflect the Lord's teaching.
Being as objective as I possibly can,
He's the standard by which one can judge a man.

～

MIKE IS MORE THAN A BOSS. He's an innovator, a motivator, and a team player. He dwells on the positive rather than the negative, yet he is realistic and honest. If I'm doing a good job, he doesn't hesitate to congratulate me. If I make a mistake, he tells me and offers constructive criticism, then moves on. It's his consistency that I rely on. I can always count on his honesty. For example, I was in charge of a project that turned into a total flop. It was one of the most embarrassing events of my entire professional career. Mike just said, "It may not have turned out the way you wanted, but you took a risk and tried something new and I admire you for that." Straightforward, challenging, supportive—he's all of these and more.

～

LINDA'S MANAGEMENT STYLE is to make every employee feel they're equal partners working toward common goals at our bank. She treats everyone the same. Everyone's contribution is valuable. Decisions are made with us, not for us or for our own good. Her flexibility extends to employees from one end of the lobby to another, regardless of position. When temperatures plummeted to minus twenty-two degrees, her concern for her own children's safety after school allowed those of us, who also had small children, to make special arrangements for our children's safe ride home.

In computer lingo it's called "WYSIWYG"—what you see is what you get. There's no question that this is the case with the bosses above. Whether these bosses are dealing with money, benefits, job expectations, or just plain human compassion, they are the same, day in and day out. They are consistent in their beliefs. They are consistent in their ethics. And they are consistently fair in the way they treat their employees. That's pretty hard to improve on in today's workplace. In letter after letter we received, employees revealed that their "perfect boss" would be one who consistently is straight with them, honest and trustworthy. They claimed that they could deal with criticism and discipline so long as the boss was honest with them. Employees want bosses they can trust.

Are We ALL Singing Out of the Same Hymnbook?

What's important to a boss? Many employees believe that the bottom line is the first and only test to the boss. In reality, employees would be surprised at how many bosses yearn for respect, acceptance, and appreciation from their workers.

What's important to employees? Bosses believe compensation and benefits are the keys to making employees happy and satisfied. Actually, many of our letters report that employees are more concerned about job security, appreciation of a job well done, and a trusting environment from nine to five.

Are bosses and their employees singing out of the same hymnbook? Not all the time. I think poor communication creates the differences. If a hypocrite is put into the mix, the lack of communication becomes a disaster. Failure to communicate is the root of many conflicts that range in scope from global confrontations to school-yard brawls. We see it daily on television programs and news interviews. Thousands of books and articles have been written on the subject of improving communication. But none of these undertakings can do as much good as a simple, clear commitment among folks to tell it like it is. If you're angry, tell your boss you're angry. If you're pleased, say that, too. But for goodness sakes, don't play games. You'll be infinitely more effective in your work and you'll totally eliminate the thousands of problems hypocrisy causes.

Some bosses use their communication skills to improve their relations with employees. Other bosses take advantage of employees with their mumbo jumbo and double dealing. The next two letters are prime examples of bosses who need to go back to communications school.

A Boss of Multiple Personalities

MY BOSS IS EXTREMELY INSECURE and has multiple personalities. One of his strongest personality traits is that of a hypocrite! He maintains he's studying to become a priest, "in case my wife dies." At the same time he is deep into pornography and discusses sexual activities frequently. He maintains he believes in the "open office" concept for good communications, but delivers loud, caustic performance reviews for other employees to hear.

He asks for his subordinates' input in a public forum. Yet, when subordinates do not agree with him, he verbally abuses them publicly, indicating they're stupid and are not "tuned-in" with his direction. He asks his employees to take the initiative in some of their work areas, and then ridicules them loudly and publicly when he feels they are attempting to undermine his authority.

He states he's the dumbest person in the office and yet he establishes the future direction for a high technology company. He hires temporary employees and tells them that he has no management skill whatsoever.

He goes on local vacation and sends an E-mail telling employees to contact him with any questions. He demands to review quotations before they are sent to customers. Yet when we call him to discuss new client quotations when he is on vacation, he delivers a five-minute tirade of how he hates his job, is going to quit on Monday, and doesn't care about the quotation. He adds we can quote it at zero dollars as far as he is concerned.

The final chapter is that I called our company president and told him I was quitting specifically because of my hypocritical boss. The next day my boss called me and said, "You're not quitting because I'm firing you!"

The Learning Curve With a Hypocrite

FIRE SOMEONE your first week on the job. Then be extra friendly with everyone else. But that's only the beginning of the ways my boss kept us off balance. His rules for employees began and ended with, "You're in charge...you write your own rules...we're a team." In effect, what happened was, "Never, never let your staff think you're not superior to them in every regard." Thus his philosophy began.

Be sure employees know about your perks: company car; reserved parking spot; bonuses; stock options; title. When possible, make comparisons aloud between your sizable bonus and theirs—all the while commenting you wish they could enjoy some of the same benefits.

Employees have regular hours, you don't. Come and go at will, after all you're the boss! Around holidays, leave at noon or even the day before. But don't be Simon Legree. Let them leave an hour early, but only if they've finished all their work.

Stress the importance of confidentiality. Then tell the department if someone's husband is out of work. Everyone should know. When you interview a particularly funny professional for a position at the company, laugh about him in front of the whole department. Show them how ridiculous he was to apply at the company in the first place. Make the employees feel special!

Most importantly, supervise all employees. Rewrite everyone's job descriptions, but don't tell them. Surprise them! You can't give them raises if they aren't doing their job correctly, right?

Don't forget the most critical issue. Only the staff makes mistakes! You do everything right. Solicit input, but take

responsibility for it, especially all the creative ideas.
Reassure them that there will be no awards for them if
you don't take the credit.
    It's been a tremendous learning curve with him. But that
bad curve is in my rearview mirror now and I'm driving
my own vehicle—in a new job!

These two bosses truly have a Dr. Jekyll and Mr. Hyde personality. It would seem to me a boss of this character is much more difficult to deal with than one who is consistently mean, because
employees have an opportunity to see at odd times the good side
of Dr. Jekyll. It's those unexpected encounters with Mr. Hyde that
keep people continually off guard. True, it's difficult to find fault
with how they appear and what they profess to believe in, but as
we see in both letters above, appearances can be deceiving.
    Here are a couple of letters from employees who have the plea-
sure of working for a WYSIWYG. Let's see what we can learn.

A Three-Way Mirror With the Same Reflection
WE ALWAYS CAN COUNT ON OUR BOSS. She's a
doctor; she's a boss; she's a friend. She has complete
responsibility for staff, patient, or procedural changes, but
she seeks our participation in decisions or changes about
our work. In a medical environment, mistakes can be critical, but she works with staff and never harshly criticizes
us if the inevitable happens.
    She works long, hard hours and yet schedules her time
off around the staff, never taking the time she is entitled to.
In fact, we are never asked to work last-minute split shifts
unless she is right there working beside us. And she makes
sure we are paid for the whole day, too.
    In spite of her heavy workload, I've seen her sit privately
with her staff or patients, who needed to talk to her—then
she stays late to finish her work. When I have asked for her
personal opinion on an issue, she never beats around the
bush. She comes straight out with a solution that I wish I
could have seen. She has a bedroom furnished at the hospital because of her irregular hours, but any staff member that
might temporarily need it is given first preference.

She is a professional and maintains that working environment, but during a personal financial difficulty, she offered to lend me a few thousand dollars with no strings attached. She also looked for things my husband could repair or build around the hospital for extra income.

She hates to drive in bad weather, but she is willing to pick up staff in snowstorms because we are all needed to handle the workload. She also sends her staff home in hurricanes whether she stays or not.

Management with Bright Lights—No Filters Needed

MY BOSS IS A BEACON in the management field and it's reflected in the operation of our hospital's medical unit and cancer care center. She expects exceptional performance from her staff, along with accountability and responsibility. She freely admits that the quality performance of her staff is the catalyst to her own success. When staff is appreciated and commended appropriately and often, she can count on hard work and self-motivation. She delegates confidently and encourages autonomy knowing that results will be high quality and a credit to her own management. Most importantly, her management style is not artificial or strictly a means for her own gain!

Each personal and professional staff request is considered by individual and situation. She looks for opportunities for employees, offers options if available, and gives directions for achieving goals if professional or personal growth is needed. She has no hidden agenda. She meets conflicts head-on and counsels when required with diplomacy and respect.

To sum it up, I heard an employee make this remark when leaving her office: "Only Lesley can call you in her office, point out flaws in your performance or character, and allow you to leave feeling good about yourself." A straight-shooter? Sure, and we love her every bullet of compassion and warmth for her employees and patients!

I guess to summarize this chapter about hypocrites and WYSIWYGs, I would stress a point I made earlier: Year in and year out we have heard employees say that the trait they seek most and appreciate the most in a boss is *straightforwardness.* They can live with having their work corrected and their performance criticized. They can deal with rejection, discipline, and failure. What they say time after time that they can't deal with is being manipulated. Unfortunately, this is the hypocrite's stock in trade.

With straightforwardness comes respect. Maybe they won't agree with what's being said or done, but they'll respect the messenger. And if you're a boss doing your job, what more can you ask for?

The Corporate Coach's Comments

You've heard the old saying, "You can't live with 'em, you can't live without 'em." Seriously, folks, a Jekyll and Hyde boss is probably unfixable unless you're a trained psychologist. But let's try anyway.

Let's divide the hypocrite boss into two categories: those who intentionally do what they do and those who can't help it. In the case of a multiple personality boss, who just can't control his mood swings, try to get ahead of the problem. Focus on controlling *your* moods and how you *react* to whatever he dishes up on any given day. When he's a bear—be patient and professional. When he's a sweetheart, be patient and professional. While you can't control him, you can always control yourself. You will not solve the problem, but you'll be able to live with it.

If your boss acts the part of a hypocrite intentionally, chances are he's trying to keep you off balance so that he can control you. In this case, the answer is probably to find a greener pasture. My reason for this goes back to the fact that intentional hypocrisy is dishonesty, and we say many times in this book that you should run, not walk, away from a dishonest boss. While you're getting away from an intentional hypocrite, keep your mouth shut and do your job as completely and competently as possible—and look for a new boss as hard as you can.

Coach's Corner

TO THE EMPLOYEE:

☞ Decide whether your boss is simply moody and, therefore, inconsistent, or whether he changes his colors to manipulate and control you.

☞ Behave consistently and professionally with a moody boss. Don't get too high during the good times or too low during the bad ones.

☞ Listen carefully to what others say–particularly your boss–and make notes just to keep the record straight and also to make sure you remember what is said.

☞ Check your own consistency score: Maybe you, not the boss, are the moving target.

TO THE BOSS:

☞ Consider whether your employees know what to expect from day to day in your management. Have you been consistent and fair in your approach and moods?

☞ Promote better communications, based on honesty, throughout the company and you will see increased employee morale and productivity in no time at all.

☞ Make sure you and your employees are singing out of the same hymnbook. Employees must know exactly what you expect of them with no hidden agendas on your part.

☞ Manage objectively, dealing with the facts and not personalities or moods.

CHAPTER 8

Buffoons and Crackerjacks

"OOPS!"..."Oh NO!"..."Aw shucks!"..."Oh H––!"...are all pretty good verbal indicators that something has gone wrong or someone has made a mistake. Unfortunately, we don't always get an advance warning when we go to work for a boss who is an "accident waiting to happen!"

We've looked at several different personality traits of bad bosses in this book, which make working for them difficult at best and nightmarish at worst. We have yet to consider the underlying intellect, skills, or ability that determine whether or not a boss is efficient or effective at his job, regardless of his personality. I believe it's time we do that because, as you will see in subsequent letters in this chapter, many bosses are criticized by their employees as being bungling, incompetent foul-ups, who routinely set into motion a series of events that create frustrated, disgusted employees.

Perhaps every manager's worst nightmare is to make a careless error that results in a disastrous mistake. Professionals work hard to avoid these terrors by maintaining a constant vigil against severe errors in judgment. Effective managers even turn these errors into learning experiences for personal growth. As we all know, however, Murphy's Law exists–mistakes happen. But those bosses are not at issue here. We also aren't discussing mediocrity and the boss who doesn't excel at anything in particular. We're talking about a manager who mishandles, mismanages, and misconducts all within his realm to the point that the workplace becomes a total disaster. In so many cases we see the business sinking and the crew looking for life rafts because the captain has the boat going in circles and can't keep his own head above water. One of my favorite quotes that we received as a contest entry was, "The only difference between this place and the Titanic is that *they had a band!*"

Let's take a look at some of the excerpts we received from employees, who must feel like crew members of their own personal "Titanic." Their bosses appear to do everything possible to flounder and provide stumbling blocks for their employees from nine to five.

OUR OFFICE CHOKED on chaos and noise. My boss's grasp of the basics–"How do you turn the computer on?"–was slippery at best. Official procedures were ignored, leaving employees to untangle and apologize. We lost money hiring her high-salaried friends to pursue doomed projects. Decisions routinely were made after deadlines, then changed and changed again. Through it all–she talked incessantly. In fact we thought she had a black belt in talking torture because her idea of a staff meeting was to have us all cook for a potluck lunch and then listen to her ninety-minute monologue.

~

OUR BOSS, the "Phantom of the Office," laboriously studied time cards and frequently made changes to reduce the actual hours, thinking employees would not remember how much time they had on the clock. The rest of his week was spent in reading newspapers, visiting with his secretary, and making personal phone calls. Annual evaluations were never done on time, if at all. He played golf every Wednesday. He couldn't operate business equipment beyond the hand-cranked adding machine. Needless to say, we had a huge turnover.

~

WITH FOUR ATTORNEYS in our law firm, it was my lot to draw the jerk! I was hired to work from 8:30 until 5:30. He comes to work at 4:30 with a list a mile long to accomplish for the day. His office is a total mess. He has files, papers, and phone messages littered everywhere. His mess is like a growing cancer that encroaches on others as he spreads out to the conference room, library, my office, and another secretary's ledge. My attempts to organize his office have met fierce resistance because "his things have to be exact." Ironically, he's fanatic about certain things. For example, staples must be put back into the exact same holes when photocopying multipage documents.

～

THE FRIGHTENING EXAMPLES of my boss's inability are endless. She keeps important papers in shoe boxes and grocery bags in her car! She refuses to use a computer as she considers them "unfriendly." She fishes through our garbage cans, pulling out paper "that's still good" and then makes me cut it all into little squares to be used for messages. She, too, works on them for hours and is "too busy" to talk to customers. She routinely forgets to make payroll deposits and the bank has started calling to remind her—yet she still forgets. The end result is that our paychecks bounce all the time.

～

I WORK FOR CLEOPATRA, Queen of Denial. She has never learned to use the computer and printer that sit at her elbow, and eschews human-made dictation equipment, preferring to use me as her personal handmaiden. She's a picky perfectionist who thinks nothing of spending an hour of her time and mine on one letter. She schedules staff meetings on Wednesdays from 10:30 to 11:30, but always starts late and continues them for two or three hours. Since Cleopatra is threatened by competence and serious input, our meetings are when her five employees merely attend the queen at court!

～

OUR POLICE CHIEF IS A DIP! He boasts that he has gotten a new building for the force, but he attended the same seminar twice on how to design a police building. The results of this studious effort are such unique features as fresh-air intakes located next to the exhaust for the diesel generator and the radio tower being constructed so close to the building that the gutters couldn't be put on the roof.

∼

I WORK IN THE SAFETY/SECURITY DEPARTMENT of a hospital, and my boss is the worst manager I've ever seen. He doesn't know how to communicate with his employees. We come out of a meeting with him and wonder what he just said. "Organization" is not in his dictionary. You can't give him anything without copying it, because it's guaranteed he will lose it 90 percent of the time. His desk is a disaster. There are five piles on his desk dating back to 1989. He waits until twenty minutes before a meeting to tell us he needs a lengthy report, although he has known about the project for weeks. He doesn't get along with other department heads, which hinders our getting things corrected or repaired. This is especially bad when you are talking safety issues.

I found myself wondering what systems were in place that allowed some of these bosses to fumble their way into management. The basic problem might have begun in the interviewing, screening, testing, and hiring processes. The fact that these bumblers ascended to the position of anyone's boss clearly indicates that there was something missing in these initial steps of employment. Occasionally, however, people may have sneaked through a job interview by overcompensating with delightful interpersonal skills, yet their day-to-day job performance always reveals the truth. We've all seen them—happy, carefree buffoons, who drive us crazy with their lack of business savvy, but who have a winsome, good-natured personality that we find hard to dislike.

The reasons that contribute to a boss's ineffective, inefficient behavior are as limitless as fish in the oceans. Some are newly promoted managers, still wet behind the ears, untrained, and unprepared for managing other people. Others are just plain careless—klutzes—who manage to muddle through the workday by repeatedly stubbing their toes. Some bosses are sloppy and could not care less that they drop the ball on project after project. There are bosses who are out of touch with the technology necessary to compete in today's business world. Then you have the bosses who, as the saying goes, aren't "brain surgeons," or "rocket scientists." They're just plain dumb! And perhaps this last group may be the most difficult for frustrated employees to work around. Let me assure you, however, as aggravating as these bosses can be, *they are in the minority.*

As we've discussed previously in this book, when a boss is recognized by upper management and promoted to a supervisory position, we assume he must have something on the ball. He indeed has impressed someone. Oh, there may be areas still unrefined in his techniques, but hopefully management training and experience will polish the edges of even the roughest diamond.

I'm the Boss...Now What?

Some people set their sights and work all their life to get the title "boss." Then what? For those who have established their goals high enough, there is a continual desire to learn and grow in the position. For bosses like those described at the beginning of this chapter, goal-setting seems to have little importance as they flop and flounder about, making their employees angry and frustrated by their lack of leadership. But as we all know, to get anywhere, you have to know where you're going, and setting professional goals helps get you there.

Experienced travelers use a road map when they begin their journey. If not, they may pass their destination and keep right on going. The traveler also needs to know the checkpoints—the distances between cities—to determine the next place to gas up. And goals form the highway to get from point A to point B, while company policies and procedures provide the various checkpoints along the way to show you the best way to get there and to monitor the trip.

Any efficient, successful manager will tell you that he has established goals not only for himself, but also for his company. He also will tell you that he guided his employees in goal-setting exercises. Goal setting requires input from many sources that influence our life—our spouse, our family, our employer, our church, and hopefully, a mentor. When we take the time and effort to establish goals for our future, we can easily see the fruits of our labor if we systematically monitor our progress along the way. It's a matter of structure, organization, and focus.

You may have the greatest, most detailed "To Do List" in the world each morning, but if you're disorganized and don't refer to it throughout the day, you may never get around to crossing even the first item off your list. How we organize our work habits is as individualistic as our personality. We get back to a person's perspective, but all of us function easier when chaos is kept to a minimum!

Organize Your Chaos

To some efficiency experts, the cardinal rule of inefficiency is to have a desk that has anything on top of it other than the immediate work at hand. A clean desk is heralded as a badge of productivity and efficiency. To others the temptation of becoming overly organized, engulfed in minutiae, is tantamount to killing effectiveness. So our goal should be to blend the best of both. We should organize as merely a means to an end.

Consider also the surroundings in which you work–your personal space. How does organizing your work area help you achieve your goals? The *location* of your work space should be conducive to performing your best work. Work areas should provide as much *comfort* as financially feasible.

As we see, there are numerous steps that we all can take to achieve a goal of efficiency and effective business practices, whether we are boss or employee. As in every journey, some travelers are farther down the road than others. The bosses described in the following excerpts are using the road map to success through efficiency and effectiveness.

THE DIRECTOR OF OUR PRESCHOOL is fair, consistent, thorough and ORGANIZED! As her office manager, I appreciate her attention to details so that our center runs smoothly, even in her absence. We all know what our job is and how to best accomplish it for the good of the families we serve. Marci is the type of boss we all hope for. She doesn't ask anything of her staff that she wouldn't do herself–from creating a curriculum to cleaning the bathrooms, and the bathrooms are always in need of cleaning!

~

SOME PEOPLE ARE UNDER THE IMPRESSION that a boss has to be tough, loud, and domineering in order to supervise staff. This is totally untrue. My boss is the superintendent of a correctional institution. He works under tremendous stress in a sometimes volatile climate. Yet he is a firm but fair disciplinarian with both staff and inmates. Critical decisions are made on a daily basis. One of his strong points is the fact that he has the gift to motivate staff and inmates alike. He took over a run-down facility and turned it into a showplace in less than a year.

∽

CRAIG IS MORE OF A MENTOR than just "boss." We've been fortunate to witness his own management skills and leadership ability. He encourages teamwork, timeliness, decisiveness, innovation, openness, hard work, courage, loyalty, even a sense of humor. These principles he not only preaches, but practices passionately. He teaches us to teach ourselves. His style isn't to have us carry out his vision, but to help us realize that we can carry out our own.

∽

MY MANAGER IS AN EXCEPTIONAL STRATEGIST. His pensive style and emphasis on strategic planning combine to position our department as one of the best in the industry. He patiently cultivates our thoughts and facilitates brainstorming sessions. As demanding as he is on goal attainment, he is pragmatic about limitations. He drives his managers to meet their goals consistently and uses his quick wit to keep us loose as we push our teams to meet the departments' challenging goals. He foresees the results of successful programs. Due to his just-in-time philosophy and elimination of non-productive activities, many manual tasks have been discontinued at our company.

∽

SOUNDS OF THE JUNGLE fill the air as the image of a rhinoceros charging through the bush appears before my eyes. "Hello Rhinos!" shouts our fearless leader as she bounds into...the jungle?...no, the conference room! "You've got to have skin as thick as a rhino's to survive the arrows shot at you out there in the jungle." Susan motivates her team with vivid analogies and raw enthusiasm.

But she is more than just a motivator and team leader; she
is a shining example of professionalism through her dress,
business manners, optimistic attitude, respectful and coura-
geous treatment of associates, and an unquenchable thirst
for knowledge and self-improvement.

The letters above reflect those cracker-jack bosses for whom we
all would love to work. When we hear about bosses who have
"razor-sharp minds," "a passion for teamwork, timeliness, decisiveness, innovation, openness, hard work," and are "shining
examples of professionalism," we know they are goal-driven
leaders who are skilled at managing people.

The descriptions of these efficient, effective bosses are vivid,
and I would like to add my own thoughts about what *leadership*
means to me. I have shared the following acronym with audiences
around the world and I hope you find it as thought-provoking as
they have.

LEADERSHIP

L Listening. They listen with an open mind to other players
and coaches.

E Empowering viewpoint. They delegate and enable others
to act.

A Ambition. They have goals, imagination, vision, as well as
ability.

D Desire. They show enthusiasm, drive, and determination.

E Example. They serve as a role model for the ideals they
believe in: honesty, common sense, and hard work.

R Respect. Leaders respect individuals and build self-esteem.

S Self-esteem. They show poise and believe in themselves,
so they don't "have something to prove" to others.

H Heart. They empathize and encourage.

I Initiative. They have the energy and ability to make things
happen.

P Patience. They are slow to criticize, quick to praise.

These truly are admirable characteristics that we find in most sea-
soned managers who are proficient, productive bosses. They are

a terrific checklist and a goal for us all to achieve. We sometimes take them for granted until we see the bosses, who make us think of the Keystone Cops in action—except the cops were funny. I think you'll agree that there's nothing amusing about the following two bosses who give the word *buffoon* new dimension.

Tag Team Clowns

WHEN MY BOSS became executive director of our nonprofit agency, his wife also needed a job. The boss immediately hired her as "interim" director, when one of our department directors took maternity leave—with a hefty 20 percent pay increase. The wife had no training or experience and was totally incompetent. While she worked at the agency, the two of them fought constantly and publicly, screaming at each other in front of staff and members. Under her "supervision" the most successful department in the entire agency went under.

The boss himself was totally incompetent. He was very secretive and locked himself in his office for most of every day. Whenever an employee asked him for anything, he always said, "I'll get back to you," but he never did. He insisted that all publicity, correspondence, and paperwork for funding agencies must go through his office, but he refused to act on anything.

When the agency began losing funding, the boss went on disability leave, claiming job-related stress. As employees went through the mess in his office in an effort to salvage the agency, we discovered his files were chaos. We found notices of overdue bills and other urgent mail—some of it several months old—unopened and buried in piles of irrelevant and unrelated papers. Shortly thereafter, half our staff was terminated in an effort to stave off impending bankruptcy directly attributable to my boss's mismanagement!

Bonehead Banker in the Lobby

WHEN HE WAS PROMOTED from cashier to loan officer, we all knew our bank was in trouble! His management style remains beyond description, although *psychological warfare* seems appropriate. He left behind a trail of frustration and maddening memories for those who worked for him.

His desk and surrounding area were monuments to his inability to make decisions. The desk was piled inches deep in neglected work and there were boxes of records strewn about like land mines.

He would teach new systems to the staff, then berate managers for being uninformed. He would withhold key information, making the managers appear inept.

He acted on every innuendo of office gossip as fact, once calling me into his office one hour before opening time and belittling me for fifty-five minutes. He then smiled sweetly and said, "You now have five minutes' rebuttal time." He treated each of us managers in an equally distasteful manner. His dislike for women was evident.

He was *a classic example of a person's being promoted to his level of incompetence!*

It appears that we merely have cracked open the lid on Pandora's box of incompetent bosses. And the ineptitude that has come flying out has been the basis for frustration and rage among employees across the country. I laughed when I read one letter that described the epitome of a disorganized boss. The employee said, "My inept boss uses an exercise routine that has our office tied in knots. He constantly *pushes his luck,* he *jumps to conclusions,* and he *dodges deadlines*—all in an effort to stay fit!" What a contrast we see, however, in the two bosses above, who are "all thumbs" when it comes to managing people, and the next two bosses, who use their thumbs with "a touch of genius," as they seem to have written the book on effectiveness as managers.

She's at Home in Business

AS AN ENTREPRENEURIAL, FOCUSED WOMAN, Claudia is a leader. She has the innate people skills that serve her well as a clear communicator and exceptional motivator. She has in-depth cross-trained talents and doesn't expect anything from others that she would and does not do herself.

A clear *mission statement* and total team concept is nurtured by Claudia, defining for each contributing person that clearly the "whole is bigger than the individual parts." A key technique she uses is true delegation, allowing the employees to think and grow with their portion of individual authority and responsibility meshed with holistic teamwork methods.

Employees find her always accessible. She gives regular feedback and public "attaboys" for major accomplishments and a simple "thanks" for the small ones. Constructive feedback always is given privately and in a supportive fashion. She is patient and doesn't overreact if employees make a mistake or take risks that miss the mark.

Claudia sets specific goals and employees do not have to guess about performance ratings. She provides positive reinforcement, and when employees aren't sure how to handle a particular project, she offers help and assures them that she knows they can do it.

What's fun is that she's an accomplished chef and never forgets a birthday with her culinary masterpieces. They are indeed a bonus from the heart of a truly "omnicompetent" lady.

A Veteran of Finesse...not War

IN THE MIDST of a corporate crisis full of layoffs, liquidations, wage freezes, and employee gloom, David managed to be an inspiration and the best boss ever! Knowledge and initiative have never been an issue. He sits at the microfiche or computer for hours, whatever is necessary to solve a problem. Although several labor grades ahead of many of us, he jumps into problems and never hesitates to get his hands dirty.

David inspires us and teaches us to persevere when it seems there is no reason to do so. He holds weekly meetings with our group over which nothing takes priority. He updates us on company news that he learns from upper-management meetings. He even got us interested in the product we do financial reporting on by playfully quizzing us on our knowledge of the product and providing guest speakers to inform us about the product.

Ours is a high-tech field where the organization is separated by functions that rarely get along. David has increased communication and understanding within our group and across functions. He motivates us and gets us excited about our jobs by asking us to present something about our work, or something helpful we have learned every week. He has increased our public speaking skills without our realizing it. This has made us feel important and confident in our abilities.

David has developed a tremendous environment at work. He has created contests and fostered a cheerful atmosphere by creating a Jeopardy-type game during lunch breaks. The end result is we look forward to coming to work because it's fun!

It appears that we've picked the cream of the crop with these two bosses, who definitely are well-versed in the facets necessary to reflect an effective leader. When I look back at the various traits that comprise the acronym on *LEADERSHIP* that we discussed earlier in this chapter, these two bosses fit the mold perfectly. In addition to their own knowledge and ability, they share with employees opportunities to grow and develop their own goals, both personally and professionally. And that's something even the "mistake prone" bosses can be schooled in—with your help.

The Corporate Coach's Comments

With the total ineptitude that we've discovered in some of these bosses, it's tempting for employees to concentrate their frustrations and to spend their energies devising tactics to get rid of the buffoons—rather than finding ways to keep them from tripping again over their own feet. Think for a moment. It could be that bosses think the disorganization and chaos at work originate with the employees and not in their own office. It could well be that the misguided goofs think they are doing what is expected of a boss. Maybe their role models were just as inexperienced as they are. And giving the benefit of doubt, what can you do to turn the situation around? How do you wind your way through the maze of chaos that your boss creates? How do you keep your job and still work for a "Cracker Jack" boss—where you not only get something good to eat when you open the box, but you also get a prize inside that makes your job fun? I'd like to recommend some opportunities for you to consider.

If no documented goals have been established for the company as a whole, or for individuals in particular, then get together with your coworkers and establish goals for your own work groups. After all, to organize the whole, you have to start with the individual parts. I did say parts—don't try to do this alone. You will need to have the "give and take" of group thinking. If your immediate boss has not been actively involved in the goal-making process, you will need his approval before implementation of your work groups. Having well-established goals is like having that good road map that we discussed earlier in this chapter. It shows you clearly where you are going, while policies and procedures show you the best way to get there.

To help the Big Boss who has trouble establishing consistent policies and procedures, write up and document the ones that are applicable to your work area and let your immediate boss share the efforts of your teamwork. By explaining to the boss that you, personally, would be a more productive, organized employee if these policies, procedures, and goals were established, you should receive not only his approval, but also his assistance.

Once you have this train rolling, your group efforts on policies, procedures, and goals may cause the "ripple effect" throughout the other departments in your company as they follow your lead. In turn, the Big Boss may be delighted to find his company is working much more efficiently and productively. If you're lucky, the boss may climb on board and like being the engineer of a well-run railroad. At this point, we don't care who takes credit for the improvement, do we?

Just be sure the boss knows there is some flexibility built into each procedure. If changing circumstances dictate an adjustment, he will probably be grateful for the "law and order" your team has brought to his firm.

REMEMBER, in your zeal to organize your environment, don't leave the impression that you are assuming your boss's authority when establishing policies, procedures, and goals for yourself. I can almost assure you that the response will be negative from the onset if you in any way threaten the boss's prestige.

REMEMBER, some bosses just aren't cut out for management, and regardless of your extensive efforts to organize things at work, they will continue to dig their own graves with their employees and in the business world. Unfortunately, in doing so, they will dig your grave as well.

Your own self-esteem and self-worth are at risk if, after painstaking elbow grease has been put into a documentation project for the company betterment, your boss fails to get with the program. At this point, you should consider cutting your losses and taking your talent and enthusiasm elsewhere. Look for a company where the boss has been around the block and has the experience and efficiency to run a successful company, as well as to have appreciation for good employees.

Coach's Corner

TO THE EMPLOYEE:

☛ Create an organized environment at your own workstation so your boss will see how much more productive you are and how much your systematic efforts add to the company's efficiency and its profitability.

☛ Document policies and procedures that affect your particular job and provide your boss a copy.

☛ Let your boss know that you look to him for knowledge and leadership in order to represent the company in the best possible light.

☛ Get off the merry-go-round and leave your boss going in circles if all your efforts fail to create a little orderliness in your company.

TO THE BOSS:

☛ Consider how your disorganized habits and lack of direction affect the efficiency of your employees and your company.

☛ Establish and write down your personal and professional goals, both short term and long range, and create benchmarks along the way.

☛ Work with your employees as they establish their own goals, and reward them at benchmark points.

☛ Provide "attaboys" and other forms of acknowledgment that employees are headed down the right road.

☛ Provide leadership in every phase of your company and you will earn the respect of not only your employees, but customers and other firms as well.

CHAPTER 9

Corporate Creeps and Good Guys

JUST AS I SAT DOWN TO WRITE THIS CHAPTER, the horrifying news came over the radio that a young businesswoman had been snatched from a parking lot, raped, murdered, and her body cast into a culvert filled with icy water from a winter's storm. The horror of this deed was compounded when the newscaster reported that 215 "known sex offenders" in the area were being rounded up for questioning.

The instant response is to lash out at our system of justice that would allow 215 convicted sex offenders to live freely in a town. One's immediate thought is to demand vengeance, seeking an eye for an eye.

A positive cycle needs to start somewhere and I am hopeful that, with this chapter, we can get rid of the Corporate Creeps from America's workplace and help eliminate potential problems that are waiting to erupt.

Sexual advances, sexist slurs, sadistic "humor"–harassment of any kind–have no place in the offices, workshops, and factories of our country, but the Best Boss/Worst Boss Contest essays tell a different tale. Witness the excerpts below.

LECHEROUS BOSSES are commonplace. I call mine an equal opportunity harasser. He's as subtle as a brick when he announces, "If you wanna keep your job, you gotta sleep with the boss." Another one of his favorite lines is, "Close the door and let me show you how much I value you." If he only knew we girls are *repulsed* by his attentions.

~

MY BOSS COMMITS SEXUAL HARASSMENT on a daily
basis. He admits it openly, but it doesn't stop him from
making remarks about going to a motel or having sex in
the park. Other employees follow his example. Recently, I
was asked a graphic and scary question: "If we beat you up
and rape you, will you tell?"

~

MY BOSS MADE SEXUAL ADVANCES on a continual basis,
usually with his tongue, while telling me what he could do
for me. The ultimate was when he appeared with his penis
hanging out of his shorts, and actually thought it would
turn me on! Needless to say, he is an ex-boss.

~

MY BOSS'S PRIORITY was getting a date. Attractive women
were hired on the spot without proper procedures. Female
clients with service complaints were soothed with, "Hi
Darlin', how's the future mother of my future kids?" He
believed his ex-wife had hired a witch to cause his failure
with women. Sometimes he ordered me to drive him to an
occultist healer on company time.

~

I WORK FOR A DOCTOR who calls the women who work
in his office "my whores." He receives lots of pornographic
magazines and videos in the mail. If he is busy watching a
porno movie, and a patient comes in, he lets the person
wait until he is through viewing the film. He loves to make
derogatory remarks about women. He called his former
office manager "worthless," and said, "All she did was think
with her crotch."

~

I USED TO WORK for an attorney. When I was hired, I did-
n't know that I was the thirty-second secretary he had hired
in less than one year. Almost immediately, I discovered he

had a habit of barging out of his office screaming, "Women, women, that's what's wrong with this world!" Needless to say, he surprised clients, waiting in the lobby, with his loud pronouncements.

~

MY BOSS TALKS ON AND ON about how women are sub-servient and only belong "home and pregnant." He makes lots of degrading comments to women in the office and is extremely demeaning to the entire staff.

~

MY BOSS IS A TRUE PSYCHO. He loves playing "psycho games" to set all our nerves on edge. The worst was the day he microwaved the mouse! The shipping manager had found a partially alive mouse on a glue pad. When the boss saw it, he put it in the microwave at break time and the first person to open the door screamed in horror, which the boss thought was hilarious.

~

INSTEAD OF A THREE-HUNDRED-WORD ESSAY for your contest, it would take at least three thousand words to describe all the hateful, horrible things my boss does. Our office is in an old building and occasionally rodents get in. We asked for traps, but the boss used poison and the rats crawled in the air ducts and died. The odor was unbear-able. The boss was annoyed that we did not appreciate his use of poison, so he set traps. When he caught one alive, he spitefully brought a garbage can half-filled with water into the office and left the rodent swimming around and around in it, until it died from exhaustion.

Sexism, sadism, and harassment are some of the most complex subjects to deal with in the workplace, since those who practice these cruelties often mask the traits with a cloak of bravado or the "humorous office clown" syndrome. In my experience over the years, it appears to me this type of unacceptable behavior gener-ally falls into one of three categories:

Type 1: The Chauvinist Pig, a man who thinks that he reigns supreme over women, calls all the shots, and can use and abuse them at will. This guy is supposed to be a thing of the past, but he's still around. Eventually, he will be rudely awakened from his fifty-year sleep when he finds himself slapped with a harassment suit, but he'll probably create a lot of pain and anguish in the meantime.

Type 2: The "WOW" Guy, who thinks he sets the females in the office on fire with his state-of-the-art wardrobe, overpowering cologne, and provocative, sexy line of chatter. His return on investment of his time and "talent" is liable to be ZERO and should give him a clue to look in the mirror and see himself as others see him.

Type 3: The Sadistic Pervert, the person who is actually happiest when he is hurting someone or something. This person can be a danger to all who cross his path.

I think one of the first thoughts one has, after reading the previous excerpts, is, "Why do the people stay and take it? What keeps them from quitting?" Contest entries almost always cited one of two prime factors: *economics* or *age*. They work in a depressed area, where jobs are hard to come by. Single mothers are afraid to quit if they are the sole breadwinner. Older employees have tenure on the job, with a pay scale that would be difficult to duplicate in the young and upwardly mobile job market. Then, let's not be coy, there are a few who actually seek this type of attention by dressing provocatively, talking suggestively, and playing the temptress on every possible occasion.

It's like coming up out of a cesspool and gulping a HUGE breath of fresh air to read about the good guys and enjoy the happy quotes of those fortunate enough to work for people of principle and character. Let's look at some of the good bosses in the following excerpts.

WHEN I MET MY BOSS a number of years ago, he was director of education for the Navajo Nation. At that time, no woman had ever been appointed to upper levels of management within the tribal structure. I did my job well and my boss valued my abilities enough to promote me to a management position. He did this against a significant political tide, since I was not only a woman, but also was white rather than Navajo. Working for him was exciting, rewarding, and filled with dignity and pride. Never once did he try to hit on me, as other bosses had. He was a true gentleman and a delight to know.

∽

MY BOSS IS A DYNAMIC VISIONARY LEADER. He is committed to excellence, not only in his work, but in his staff, as well. He encourages us to greater heights of responsibility in our jobs than we thought possible. He goes out on a limb to help his staff with their priorities. Last year, at the end of my pregnancy, I realized I could not bear the thought of someone else raising my child, but I couldn't afford to quit work. I asked my boss if a work-at-home situation would be possible. Not only was he extremely helpful, but he was the driving force behind getting all the bureaucracy of the state university where we worked to approve the policy. In the state environment, he is setting trends on behalf of his staff.

∽

WHEN MY BOSS BECAME PRESIDENT and CEO of the savings and loan where I worked, he spent the first several months finding out about his employees' strengths and abilities. He then moved people into positions where he felt they could reach their potential, be happy, and benefit both themselves and the company. He didn't see the lack of a college degree as a hindrance, but encouraged obtaining as much education as possible and willingly spent the company's money toward this end. He believes in complimenting us when we are doing a good job and does so often. He is never prejudiced. He believes ALL individuals, no matter what the color or gender, must be treated fairly.

∽

STARTING A NEW JOB is bad enough, but having to get to know a new boss is frightening, when you have just left a boss who verbally beat you into the ground. My new boss must have a loving and giving mother and an equally wonderful wife. They both gave him the best instruction in regard to treating women. He notices when I wear a new dress. He always says "please" and "thank you," even for the smallest thing. He has made me feel unique and a worthwhile person. Most importantly, he has given me confidence in myself.

∼

OUR OFFICE STAFF consists of five females. The one quality I admire most in our boss is the *respect* he gives to each one of us. Working for him is a pleasure. It is often difficult to keep an office balanced, when it comes to one male and five females. His thoughtfulness and imagination work overtime to keep everyone happy. He has a wonderful sense of humor and his words of thanks and praise to the staff are a daily occurrence. He is the best boss one could have.

∼

MY BOSS MAKES COMING TO WORK A PLEASURE. She is sensitive about workers' private lives. When I adopted a baby, she created a flexible schedule for me. Because of my religious beliefs, I do not celebrate Christmas. Not wanting to exclude anyone from celebrations, she left a beautifully wrapped gift on my desk, for Groundhog Day! She has found the balance between professional distance and friendship. She is close enough to her staff that we respect and love her, yet not so close that she can't give constructive criticism of our work. She expects excellence, yet encourages us not to dwell on mistakes. Her emphasis is on accomplishment and team effort.

If you contrast the *productive energy* of the bosses recorded in the above excerpts and the *destructive energy* of the creeps at the beginning of this chapter, the difference is so enormous that it is difficult to comprehend how a company would allow even one corporate creep to operate within its walls.

Big Bucks Down the Drain

When you actually put a dollar figure on the negative baggage the creeps carry with them, you will find it is substantial. They spend valuable company time planning and executing their sexual fantasies, while keeping female workers figuratively, and sometimes literally, "on the run." Similarly, a psycho, who totally disrupts the workforce with his shenanigans, definitely has a strong negative influence on the productivity and overall success of a company.

The following two letters are prime examples of the havoc that a tremendous ego—with a twisted sense of values—can create throughout a company, when a boss treats employees with a total lack of compassion or personal regard.

Chauvinist...and Proud of It!

MY FORMER BOSS is the worst imaginable! This female-harassing, midlife crisis, self-idolizing man has wreaked havoc on many with his cruel concept of what a boss should be. He thinks the only place for women is at his feet or in his bed.

At his company, men were never allowed to answer the phone, that was woman's work. At the office he proudly wore a small gold pendant shaped like a woman's lower private part, and shared numerous pictures of his travels to various nudist colonies in the Bahamas.

He hated children and once yelled at me, "I don't care if your brats eat TV dinners every night, you'll stay until the job's done!" I was a successful account executive and knew what areas of my job were critical. What he suggested made no sense, it was just one more way of forcing his will.

At Christmas, the boss would share the company wealth by giving each employee a fifty-dollar bill. One employee was giving birth and couldn't be at the office to receive her fifty-dollar "bonus" in person. She had to forfeit the money. "Those were the company rules," he said.

He did care enough to call each day from his favorite bar—five minutes before closing time to make sure we were still there! My ideal boss? One who shows me respect!

A Peach Pit of a Boss

OUR BOSS IS A PEACH—a peach pit, that is! As dictatorial lord and master of a county agency with a finely tuned manner of discriminating against women and bullying women and men alike, I feel he is a shoo-in to win the title as the worst boss of the year.

My boss on working mothers: "You don't plan to run off and have a baby, do you?"

My boss on women in construction: "Now, you're not going to run home crying the first time a contractor cusses in front of you, are you?"

My boss on women's clothing: "That dress doesn't do a thing for you. Now that blue one said a lot to me."

My boss on communication with his staff: He reduced two coworkers (one male, one female) to tears through ridicule. When I disagreed with him, he swore at me several times and told me not to offer an opinion, unless he asked for it.

My boss on workplace morale: One of our city's professional sports teams made it to the finals. The entire town went all out and everyone wore team shirts. Because our boss had not come up with the idea first, he posted notices that team wear would not be acceptable, because such attire "reflects poorly upon the professionalism of the department."

There is no question, the bosses portrayed in these two letters are complete losers. Bosses who play the "warlord" with their employees will often attempt to use similar tactics with customers or clients, particularly if they are female. Goodwill is foreign to them.

After wading through the sleaze and negative values of the previous creepy bosses, it's a true delight to read the appreciative letters from employees whose bosses reflect respect and integrity. The next two letters definitely restore one's faith in mankind.

A Boss Who's "Gender Blind"

FOR MOST MEN, relocating your family and your career to the United States from South Africa would be a formidable challenge, indeed. Not so for Roy, who was unable to further tolerate the social injustices perpetrated in his native homeland.

Associating himself with a firm in this country, Roy did not "do as the Romans do." Rather, he implemented his own brand of ethics and integrity at the company. He wisely made minor changes at first, then gradually became the innovator of numerous major improvements for office and industrial workers alike.

Roy had risen to vice president of finance and administration at the company when he hired me as his secretary. With only basic typing skills acquired during high school, Roy described me as a "diamond in the rough." To upgrade this image, he sent me to numerous word processing, management, communication, and negotiation seminars.

Roy was "gender blind." He would not tolerate discrimination in any form, regardless of age, religious background, sex or sexual preference. To him, "head of household" and "single parent" was asexual and synonymous. He understood when my children were ill, because you see, his children were sometimes ill, too.

If Roy had not served as my mentor, I have no doubt that this "diamond" would have unquestionably remained a lump of coal. I will forever be in his debt.

Gone Are the "Good Old Days"...Thank Heavens!

IN THE '70s in Texas, there were very few women executives. The "good ol' boy" network subjugated most females to clerks, typists, and secretaries. We were called "Darlin', Honey, Sugar, and Sweetie." We had our bottoms pinched and patted and we performed every menial task the "good ol' boy" didn't want to do for himself.

In 1980, after enduring many "creepy, biased bosses," I was privileged to work for David. He treated me as a person with a brain. From the first day we met, David assumed I was intelligent and competent. I was an on-site property manager and David never made surprise visits to check up on me. He never second-guessed my decisions. He trusted me and valued my judgment.

David encouraged me to continue my education in my field and supported me unconditionally. When I was terrified of taking a very technical financial course, he became my cheerleader and boosted my confidence. His confidence and trust in me greatly enhanced my self-esteem and motivated me to do the best possible job.

David is a warm, caring, funny person, a dedicated family man, and the most intuitive male I have ever had the pleasure of knowing.

To me, the most important quality in a boss is the respect he gives his employees. David never once considered my sex. He respected me as a person, for which I will always be thankful.

See what I mean about "restoring one's faith in humankind"? These are thoughtful bosses of sterling character, who make positive things happen for their employees and their companies. In return, they enjoy emotional and financial success generated by cheerful, productive players who willingly work as a team—with their greatest goals being a happy boss and a successful company.

The Corporate Coach's Comments

It is important that everyone in the company—from the boss on down—acts and dresses in a professional manner. This will not only improve the company's public image, it will help make the working environment one in which each person feels comfortable. You may even be able to avoid some undesired situations by not inviting misunderstanding in the first place. The fact is, however, that most harassment is unsolicited and you may well find yourself in a situation over which you feel that you have little control. In most cases, however, you really are not powerless.

Start by clearly and unambiguously letting those around you know when something they do is offensive to you. You don't need to yell or threaten, just let them know in a friendly way that whatever they're doing makes you feel bad. Is your boss in the habit of telling you off-color jokes or stories? Do you laugh and appear to encourage these stories even though you don't like them? Do you go so far as to return a similar one of your own? If you are more worried about "fitting in" than about being respected, even a reasonable boss might never understand how you feel. Creeps certainly won't. If someone should touch you in a way that you feel is inappropriate, you must immediately, firmly, and clearly tell them that this is unacceptable behavior.

Another tactic is to try to avoid being alone with someone who might be potential trouble. When you see the peacock preening his feathers and sauntering your way, take evasive action. Go to a coworker's desk and start a conversation about a job-related topic. Make your way to the rest room. Take your lunch or coffee break, preferably with another employee, not alone.

If harassment continues in spite of the fact that you have clearly indicated that you want it stopped, your next step is to tell the harassor that if he or she (yes, it happens) doesn't stop, you will take formal action. If this doesn't work, and you work for a fairly large company, you should then contact your human resources director. I can't guarantee that you'll get a fair hearing, but your chances are pretty good. Most companies today are finally beginning to get the picture and are increasingly intolerant of harassment. You will have a better chance if you have handled the harassment in a professional manner and have not started a lot of gossip, instituted an underground rebellion, generated discontent among your coworkers, or otherwise appeared to be a "trouble-maker."

Finally (or sooner if you work in a small office), you can contact your local (municipal or state) human rights or human relations commission. Their number will be in the telephone directory. If this still doesn't work, your utlimate action is either to leave the job or hire an attorney–neither one a happy solution. Only you can make that decision.

If, by chance, you have a "Type 3" *pervert boss*, it probably would be best to resign from your job immediately without any confrontation on your part. Unstable, sexual abusers are very dangerous and need trained professionals, rather than amateurs, handling their case.

Coach's Corner

TO THE EMPLOYEE:

☞ Analyze objectively your business wardrobe and your behavior to make sure that you aren't inadvertently encouraging unwanted attention from your boss.

☞ Maintain a professional atmosphere when your boss is around and don't encourage off-color stories and jokes. By all means, don't succumb to telling dirty jokes yourself.

☞ Pay attention to the "early warning signs" of the office Don Juan and make yourself scarce when you seen him preening his feathers for the next advance.

☞ Notify superiors if sexual harassment continues in spite of your efforts.

☞ Protect your reputation and your safety and don't stay in an environment when you are placed in a compromising position. Look for work elsewhere if your efforts fail to rectify a harassment problem.

TO THE BOSS:

☞ Look in the mirror and see yourself as others see you. For bosses who fit this chapter, grow past the Don Juan, Loverboy image. You now have a great deal more to give your company and your employees than a suggestive leer or an unwanted kiss in the elevator.

☞ Take your talent for business and mix it with generous amounts of courteous treatment of all your employees, regardless of sex, race, ethnic background, or religious preferences.

☞ Discover, as hundreds of companies have, that business*women* bring a new dimension to your company and treat them with the respect they deserve.

☞ Use the team approach in your company to include all employees. I can assure you the payback will be an abundance of loyal customers, happy, productive employees, and a much better chance of financial success.

CHAPTER 10

Con Artists and Honest Abes

BASED ON OVER FORTY YEARS OF EXPERIENCE in management and my many years of conducting the "Best Boss/Worst Boss" contest, I can absolutely, positively say without reservation that there is one trait which, without fail, makes a bad boss out of anyone. That trait is dishonesty. No matter what other redeeming features a boss may have, no matter how impressive the successes or rewards, if a boss is dishonest, he is a bum and he will fail.

Now, you may be wondering why I am being so tough on this issue. Well, it's because there is nothing that a boss can do that will totally destroy his business, his reputation, and the morale of his employees faster than dishonesty. I have seen great businesses, and supposedly great bosses, whose success seemed imminent, completely fall apart when employees, customers, and partners finally realized that they could not believe what the boss was saying.

I had a personal experience with a dishonest boss early in my working career. He set some very lofty and almost impossible goals to make and he promised that if the goals were attained, I would receive a substantial raise and bonus. Much to his surprise, we did make it and—you guessed it—he had a sudden case of amnesia, and I didn't receive the bonus or the raise. Because of this dishonest boss, I lost complete confidence and trust in him and I chose to leave the company shortly afterward.

I'm not the only one to discover the importance of being able to trust a boss. When a boss lies to an employee, he is saying by his actions that he doesn't respect that individual. Of course it works the other way, too. An employee who is not honest with the boss is showing a lack of respect for the boss, both personally and professionally. Without respect, relationships will fail–including the relationship between a boss and employees.

Our letters have reported many types of dishonest bosses ranging from blatant, pathological liars to those who skillfully mislead with wisps of truth where clear statements of fact are needed. Some even carry their dishonesty to the next level when they cheat, victimize, and defraud their employees. Let's look at a few examples.

WHEN AN ELDERLY COUPLE committed suicide in one of our apartments, my boss took their bed out of the apartment even before their burial! He told his secretary the bed was perfectly good and should be "put to good use." When the public fiduciary's representative inquired about the missing bed, my boss immediately said someone had stolen the bed...through the eighteen-by-forty-eight-inch window. He blamed the police department for leaving the windows open to air out the place!

∾

MY BOSS IS A PRINCIPAL without principles! He lies to protect himself and to please everyone. He tells people what they want to hear even if it contradicts what he has already told someone else. He blames the administration for not acting upon requests when, in truth, those requests are swallowed by the black hole he calls his desk.

∾

MY BOSS IS A REAL LOW-LIFE! He "whites out" his sales representatives' names on contracts they have sold. He puts his name in their place to look good with his boss and to reduce the commission split with us at the end of the month. He actually has the gall to sarcastically thank every employee for having a bad month, but always takes credit himself for every good month.

∾

MY FORMER BOSS was a poisonous snake, a chameleon, and a pathological liar! Uncontrollable lies slipped through his teeth like venom. He was ruthless and reckless. He was plagued with an incurable virus that he spread to his management team and to other employees. He falsified performance appraisals, sabotaged my work, instructed employees to alienate me, and spread rumors to employees, business associates, neighbors, and friends that I was mentally ill. The biggest irony: He was a human resource director of a major corporation.

∼

LITTLE DID WE REALIZE that the handsome body with the friendly smile housed the soul of a rattlesnake and the conscience of Damion. Our new publisher decided to make us "real producers" by calling and lying to our clients that we had quoted them wrong advertising prices. He made special deals with lower prices and cheated us by cutting our commission to compensate for the reduced revenue. Once when I won a trip to New Orleans for top advertising sales, I went to pick up my tickets three months later only to discover that my boss already had used them. When I confronted him, he lied and told me I had waited too long. "After all," he lied, "the tickets were valid for only a year!"

∼

I LEARNED THE CONCEPT of management by deceit from the owner of a gas station where I worked for three years. He lied to the public about whether or not our public rest rooms were available. To those travelers just passing by and needing only a rest stop, a permanent, handwritten sign read, "Out of Order." To paying customers wanting to use the rest room, he shouts, "It's okay now! They just told me the plumber fixed the rest rooms this morning." He was just as deceptive to employees. He lied about anything that served him at the time.

∼

HE'S A WELL-RESPECTED ORTHODONTIST but, to employees, he is the most dishonest boss on earth. Our personal belongings mysteriously vanish. One employee was missing a dress; another, a birthday card. Both were mailed to the office from their mothers. The dress was found in my boss's bathroom. The card was on his desk. Once an employee was leaving on vacation and requested her paycheck early. He pretended to call the bank for a loan, insisting he didn't have the money. I'm his bookkeeper and I know the account contains thousands of dollars at all times.

I decided to include so many examples of letters about lying bosses because I wanted to stress how many different ways there are to be dishonest. Unfortunately, it doesn't come in just one flavor.

Now, we all know what a plain old lie is. It's anytime you don't tell the truth. But that's only part of the test. It is also dishonest if you leave the person you are speaking to with the wrong impression. The question isn't necessarily whether you have said anything that is not true, but whether the listener has heard anything that is not true. In other words, honesty isn't always judged by what the speaker *says*, but rather by what the listener *hears*. I think Half-truth Harry and Tony the Truth-Twister will help me make my point.

Half-Truth Harry

Let's face it, most folks are pretty smart. They figure out after a while when a person is lying to them and learn to deal with it. But the toughest type of dishonest boss to deal with is one who says just enough to sound like he's telling the whole story, but leaves out a few well-chosen items that make all the difference. You know the type. What always has amazed me about these people is where they find the time to create and refine the "scripts" they use for their deceptions. Yet we run into them time after time at our jobs.

Once you encounter a person who engages in this type of deceitful behavior, it is essential that you let him know that you are not willing to be a party to such games. Listen carefully. Ask the Half-Truth Harry to repeat himself. Ask for explanations. Ask for clarifications. Take notes. Somehow you must take up the defensive position of proving to yourself beyond any doubt that you fully understand the message being communicated.

Tony the Truth-Twister

Another type of dishonesty is that in which the facts are twisted to leave you with the wrong impression of reality. Now, dealing with a truth-twister is even more difficult than dealing with a person who tells half-truths, because no matter what you say, a truth-twister will reform it to his purpose. On the other hand, a Half-Truth Harry will never tell the rest of the story, if questioned. In my experience there is no way of dealing with a person who twists the truth, therefore, you need to find a way to twist your way out of any job situation that tolerates a truth-twister.

I don't think you'll see a Half-Truth Harry or Tony the Truth-Twister in the following bosses. I do think you'll see that employees appreciate these honest bosses, who put all their cards on the table and never deal from the bottom of the deck.

ONCE MY BOSS AND I were at a market and someone had dropped a ten-dollar bill. Instead of putting it in her pocket, she gave it to the store manager and asked him to find the person who dropped it. This same honest, giving attitude comes into our workplace. When you work in this kind of atmosphere, sales rise, smiles heighten, and teamwork is taken to a new dimension. What more can I say than this: "Wouldn't you like this caring, honest woman as your boss?"

~

MY BOSS IS ONE OF THE MOST POSITIVE, straightforward, uplifting people I have ever had the opportunity to work for. He points out your strong points and teaches you how to handle different situations. I can describe him best by his favorite saying, "*It's not who's right...but what's right!*"

~

TODAY I AM A BETTER MANAGER because of Louie's guidance. His honesty and integrity are unmatched and when combined with his other leadership qualities, have provided me with the best boss in the world. He sets the pattern for everyone to emulate in our Fortune 500 company. I happily would do anything the man asked because I know I will get 100 percent of the credit, and no matter how good I make him look, he makes me look even better.

≈

MAGGIE HAS THE UNENVIABLE JOB of keeping three-hundred-plus employees on the path, striving for improved patient care at a large county hospital. That alone should earn her a gold medal, but that's just the beginning. She's honest, fair, tough, self-determining with strong principles that she lives by and expects others to mirror. She is an "esteem builder" rather than an "esteem demeaner," and all her employees are richer because she brings out the best in her staff.

≈

KARL IS MY *SILVER LINING* to my previous *dark cloud* bosses. He's fair and honest. He wouldn't think of stealing our work or ideas for himself and is our biggest fan. He also understands that we "work to live and not live to work."

≈

WHAT CAN I SAY about a person who instilled values into my life, but the truth. My boss, Joe, was the most sincere, compassionate, understanding person I've ever met. He took the time to teach me to set honest goals. He was and still is a respected and knowledgeable businessman in our community and a leader who is admired by his employees. We willingly travel in his path, following his example.

You will be amazed at how much more efficient and successful you will be if you don't have to waste 40 percent of your energy every day trying to create or decipher half-truths and twisted tales. Honesty is not only the best policy, it is the only policy.

Criminal activity and pending litigation were two automatic disqualifiers for our annual contest, but numerous employees "vented" about these issues regardless of the fact they would not win. Therapeutic value outweighed a trip to Hawaii in many cases. The two bosses described next are two such examples, but they epitomize dishonesty in rare form.

A Deceiver's Unwilling Accomplice

NOT ONLY DOES MY BOSS LIE, but *he makes me lie for him.* And that's the worst! He makes me lie to his wife about his whereabouts. I'm to tell her that he is at a client's office, when she can see him through his office window because she phones from the pay phone across the street. She yells at me, telling me she can see him, and he still has me insist that she is wrong, it's not him.

When he celebrated his wedding anniversary, he sent me out (with his car) to a boutique several blocks away for a gift for her. Because she tracks the exact mileage on his car, he had me drive the car *backwards* so the odometer reading was not off by the slightest fraction.

When clients or bill collectors call enraged to talk to him about a mistake or an outstanding bill, he makes me lie to them, saying his father has passed away. One client responded, "This is the second time in ten months his father passed away. Put the jerk on the phone!"

It never fails that when he orders lunch from a nearby restaurant, the man never has the money to pay the delivery boy. I nearly have gone broke feeding him, yet, he always promises to reimburse me—but he never does! What's worse, he asks me for the receipt for the food. Then he goes to the restaurant the next day and tells the owner that I lost the receipt, so he can deduct the lunch *twice* as expenses.

A Charlatan in Boss's Clothing

MY BOSS OWNS A TEXTILE COMPANY and dresses himself in deceit—not our products. There is no end to his shenanigans. Instead of being paid for our annual holidays as they occur throughout the year, he pays them in one lump sum the beginning of December. The pay equates to eighty hours of income for the employees. One week prior to Christmas, he announced that he could only pay half and would pay the remainder as soon as feasible. It's June and still no money, and no word as to if we will ever get it!

He also started a 401(K) plan, to which he has matched an overwhelming ZERO! In fact, not only has everyone who invested lost money, but our payroll stubs indicate no

money has been put into the plans for three months.
Instead, the money is being used by the boss.

He also has a reputation for not paying his creditors,
including property taxes. It's finally beginning to catch up
with him, because our customers are dropping like flies,
not to mention employees leaving by the droves.

Working for a liar is bad enough, but being made an unwilling
accomplice is unforgivable. After reading these two letters, my
only recommendation to an employee who works for a con artist
of this magnitude would be to look for another job immediately.

Many letters that we received commented about good bosses
whose integrity was never an issue. It's the foundation of who
they are. Their honesty and how they deal truthfully with people
is just taken for granted. It definitely is the case with the next two
bosses, who obviously practice what they preach; but as we see,
they don't preach.

A Mover and Shaker with Integrity

ROB'S MANAGEMENT STYLE consists of openness, *honesty*, fairness, and a sense of humor. Each employee at our
travel service is urged to explore all possibilities, to set no
limits, and to rely on individual employee integrity. Rob
sets the pace for us, showing appreciation and full support.

A thank-you note is written on every paycheck, along
with generous sincere verbal praise. He also promotes
employee-of-the-month recognition. Does our staff have
positive self-esteem? You betcha!

Putting his heart and soul into everything he does to make
a real difference in the quality of peoples' lives, Rob is an
excellent role model. He is a mover and shaker in countless
civic endeavors and continually displays his concern for
human welfare, the welfare of the community, and the welfare of his staff.

A Boss Who Gives Credit Where Credit is Due

MY BOSS, WAYNE, is so secure in his own considerable expertise that he is not threatened by competence in
others. This is the quality I prize most in a boss.

When I came on board, he allowed me the independence to build programs and establish procedures. "I have to listen to people's ideas," I once heard him say, "because their ideas are good." But we don't always see eye to eye. He initially opposed one of my projects. Later, in spite of his earlier reservations, he did support it with his own suggestion. When the plan produced results, he took none of the credit himself. Instead, he recommended me for a promotion. That's true confidence and a wonderful example of how a boss of *integrity* should be!

There's not a lot that I can add to the displays of integrity in the two bosses described above. They have discovered that honesty is not only the best policy, it is the only policy.

The Corporate Coach's Comments

Dishonesty is such a fundamental flaw that there is no circumstance under which you should continue to work for a dishonest person.

Coach's Corner

TO THE EMPLOYEE:

☛ Think before you speak and make sure that you don't mislead anyone, especially your boss, by half-truths, distortions, or twisted facts. These are worse than no communication at all.

☛ Listen carefully and take notes, if necessary, to make certain you understand the boss's directives.

☛ Be aware that it's not what you say, but what the listener hears that is the test of honesty.

☛ Leave illegal activities and criminal behavior in the hands of the experts. Don't take on a boss with a criminal mind, because you will suffer the "fallout."

TO THE BOSS:

☛ Take care not to mislead employees, because a boss's credibility is based on honesty. Employees won't long follow a dishonest boss.

☛ Learn to listen for what's not being said, as well as what is said, particularly in dealing with employees.

☛ Create an atmosphere of trust in your company so that employees can confide in you regardless of the situation. Employees sometimes shade the truth if they are afraid of their boss.

☛ Set an example for your team to earn their respect, because employees will go to the mat for a boss they admire and trust.

CHAPTER 11

Tasmanian Devils and Cool Dudes

LOOK AROUND YOU. There is often a great deal of unhappiness and personal distress in the world because people don't always control tempers, appetites, passions, and impulses. "I wish I hadn't said that." "Oh, if only I had stopped myself." "I'd like to relive the last four hours." These are all too familiar refrains. I've said them myself, haven't you? Rare indeed is the person who at times doesn't wish for more self-control, more thoughtfulness, better *discipline*. What a wonderful world it would be if our emotions were always under control! Wouldn't we all like to work in a place where there was no stress, no deadlines, no difficult situations, and no troublesome people? I know I would. But we all deal with stress, with people, and with situations differently.

A couple of centuries after his death, George Washington's school notebook was discovered at Mount Vernon. There, hidden away for years, were fifty-four "Rules of Civility" that our first president scripted to describe the way men should treat other men. Each thought contained a wealth of George's wisdom, but one in particular bears repeating:

> *Think before you speak; pronounce not imperfectly or untruthfully; do not bring out your words too hastily, but orderly, honestly and distinctly.*

Self-discipline and control were emphasized in Washington's day, and the need is just as important today—particularly in business.

The excerpts below describe bosses who are anything but "civil" to their employees.

I WAS JUST A KID out of college, eager to start working, and was excited to be hired as his legal assistant. Little did I know that his office would become a torture chamber and that my boss would unfold into some-one we called "The Tasmanian Devil." Taz's most visible personality trait was his barbaric temper. More than once, I witnessed law books thrown within inches of hitting me. On more than one occasion during his tantrum he put all the phones on "hold." I remember a client coming to the office when he couldn't get through and asking if the phones were broken. With fists pounding loudly on the conference table, Taz screamed "Damn it! Can't I even take the phones off the hook if I want to?"

～

MY BOSS'S TEMPER TANTRUMS and outbursts are a daily occurrence. No one is safe. We all cringe when we hear his keys jangling each time he comes in the office. We even alert each other to his arrival. "The evil one is coming!" spreads like wildfire when he's been spotted. He spits when he yells, and the louder he yells, the higher his voice gets, until his veins bulge. He has gone on rampages over too strong coffee, uncovered brownies, and a phone ringing more than twice. He is the president and sole stockholder of our company, so these confrontations are inescapable.

～

THE TENSION IN THE AIR was oppressive when my boss was present. He would stalk the showroom floor as the sales force scattered, trying to look busy. This employee flight was for good cause. His temper tantrums have included throwing log books across the showroom floor, the total destruction of a plywood and Plexiglas display rack with a sledge hammer in the middle of our parking lot, and the turning over of a large metal sales desk that was in the corner of our show-room while customers and employees looked on in amaze-ment. There were reminders everywhere of his previous flare-ups, including a hole in a door made when he lost his temper with a finance manager and slammed his fist into it.

PICTURE THE CEO of a market leader, patrolling the hallways, searching out his underlings for abuse while holding in his hand and rolling back and forth, hand to hand, that simple child's toy–a Slinky. As his temper rose and his face reddened, the Slinky went faster and faster. Much like the mad captain in the *Caine Mutiny,* one can judge his mood by watching the facial tics, the red crimson face, and the pace of the distinctive metallic twang of his toy. One day something caused him to blow up at our sales manager and he grasped the Slinky and flung it viciously across the warehouse floor, bounding off the west wall, back to the east corner and landing limply in the center. Shocked, we all looked at his lifeless bit of metal and before anyone could react, he stalked off like an infantile junior high schooler.

MY BOSS'S OUT-OF-CONTROL TEMPER TANTRUMS are an everyday event. He starts by slamming doors, kicking boxes, throwing books, and tossing things around the office. He swears and yells and stomps around the office and warehouse. The temper tantrums are usually over something terribly traumatic–like a fax not going through or he's misplaced something.

ONE MORNING I CAME TO WORK to find my office in total disarray. Papers were scattered, files were turned inside out, and computer disks were thrown throughout the room. When asked what happened, my boss said, "The printer's out of toner!" She watched while I spent several hours putting my office back together. When I was sick, I took my doctor's release back to her. She yelled, crumpled it up, and threw it, hitting me in the forehead.

NEVER IN MY WILDEST DREAMS did I think I would get the opportunity to acknowledge the worst boss in the world.

God, I love this country! My boss has eighty-plus employees who report to him. On a mild day, he takes his bad temper out on the computers. If he doesn't get desired results, he pounds on the keyboard and keys fly everywhere. There was a particularly bad day when he tried to call into a certain area code and kept getting a busy signal. He became wild-eyed and ripped the phone out of the wall!

There is a significant difference between a boss who isn't always the example of tactfulness and one who loses his temper and raises his voice to an employee. There is also a vast difference between a boss who occasionally yells at people and a boss whose tirade results in objects flying through the air and expensive office equipment being broken. These letters are clear examples of bosses who need to stop and consider the psychologist's advice to those who lose their temper at the drop of a hat.

> *Step back and take a deep breath.*
> *Count to ten. Think of the conse-*
> *quences of your words and actions.*
> *Smile. Proceed slowly with self-control.*

That's easy for him to say. I wonder just how many times these consultants have encountered a boss or an employee who blows his stack and a fiery temper erupts that makes Mt. Vesuvius seem like a tempest in a teapot. But the advice is sound, and unquestionably many volatile situations can be defused by a little self-control.

Mind Over Matter

I've actually seen managers who practice their own version of this instruction in self-discipline. One manager in particular, who does not have an easygoing temperament by nature, told me, "Coach, if I feel a blowup coming on, I just excuse myself, turn and walk away. It may appear rude to some people, but it beats the alternative. I just concentrate on something or someone else and return to the situation or person when cooler heads prevail." It works for him. Whatever technique we employ, it's important that we find a method to soften whatever tendencies we have to fly off the handle at times of stress and anger. We've heard this statement countless times: "It's just a focus of mind over matter." Unfortunately, many people who have a naturally *short fuse* never worry about nor consider the consequences of a tirade directed at a coworker or an employee. Working relationships are stretched tighter than a thin rubber band by the fallout of such hotheadedness. People, like elephants, have long memories. Once exposed to someone with a volatile temper, most of us are cautious in our encounters with the individual in the future. A comfortable, relaxed relationship is seldom possible, because you never know exactly what will set off another fit of rage. Trust me, controlling your temper and practicing a little tolerance at work will do wonders for the relationships, particularly those between bosses and employees, and you will feel better about yourself!

"Thar She Blows!"

Like many things in life, patience and self-control do not come easily to most of us. In a continuing fear of a world that's passing us by too quickly, we want everything now—not tomorrow.

We rush from one year to another, eager for the next birthday and the opportunities it brings until middle age brings reflections of "the good old days." We rush each morning to get to work, eager to complete as many projects as possible during the day, so that we can hurry home to be with our family in the evening. We start the next morning again in a dead rush, gulping down cup after cup of black coffee just to get the juices flowing to go to work, and the circle never ends. It's the age we live in. We rush about seeking fulfillment and success only to find the inevitable pressure and stress that are interrelated. What we also find along the way are frustration and anger. Then at some point, we reach the boiling point. The next thing we know—"thar she blows"—with an explosive outburst of temper that sometimes surprises even ourselves.

I've always admired those people who seem to be blessed with the "patience of Job." I've known some who elevate tolerance and self-control almost to an art form, because literally *nothing* "gets under their skin." How do they do that? Do they give lessons to people in the business world? The bosses described next could conduct their own classes on patience. They've mastered the art of maintaining their "cool," and look at how it affects their employees.

I DOUBT THAT THERE IS A NEGATIVE BONE in Max's body. He keeps his cool and tries to help employees see both sides of an issue, without making us feel small or like imbeciles. He is quick to laugh and look on the bright side, even though he is serious about our business and the bottom line. He can admit if he's made a mistake, and empowers me to make my own decisions by helping me to think situations through. He listens and allows me to blow off steam if that is what I need. If imitation is the sincerest form of flattery, I hope someday to be a manager just like Max.

～

EVERYONE LOVINGLY REFERS TO OUR BOSS as Mr. S. He is kind, thoughtful, considerate, and soft-spoken. Mr. S is a gentleman in the truest sense of the word. Even if a secretary makes a mistake, he doesn't belittle her. He treats employees with respect and dignity. Many times when I am leaving for the day, he will make a point of saying, "Thank you for your help today." My response is always that it's my pleasure to do his work.

～

WE AFFECTIONATELY CALL HER "Boss." She always has a smile and time for her employees. I remember thinking, during the first couple months of employment, how she effectively managed people exactly like I had been taught in a leadership class. She deals one-on-one with all situations in a fair manner, whether the circumstance is good or bad. The work atmosphere is pleasant, and I have never detected elevated stress levels from "Boss" or any of the employees. In fact, should an employee leave their job for any reason, it isn't uncommon for them to ask to be rehired somewhere down the road.

∾

IN OUR OFFICE no one complains about the boss. Sidney is
kind, sensitive, caring, and thoughtful to all his employees.
Although he's an attorney and a bankruptcy trustee presid-
ing over a caseload of three thousand with a staff of twelve,
he always takes time to show a personal interest in us and
our families. He's willing to patiently listen to personal or
professional problems or any suggestions regarding office
procedures. Sidney is the personification of a best boss
because his proven theory is that if you keep your employees
happy, they will be loyal and productive. He's a keeper!

∾

WE CALL HER "BOSS," counselor, friend, "mama." She
has a ready smile that makes you want to continue to try
to finish a job in adversity—even on the "Mondays from
h——." I've never seen her lose her "cool" and she is
always quick to praise and recognize a job well done.
She's an effective teacher when your performance is not
100 percent and doesn't make you feel stupid if you don't
know the answer or can't spell a medical word. Medical
people do speak a language all their own, you know. She
brings out the best in all of us and believe me, this is no
small feat, if you knew some of our staff!

∾

THE BEAUTY OF ARVIN'S PERSONALITY is apparent
before one even enters our place of business. That beauty
is personified in the multicolored hues of the blooming
pansies in our office's rock garden, which is Arv's pride
and joy. His sense of humor is displayed by his three
tomato plants, "Tom," "Dick," and "Harry," with whom he
has asked each of us to converse in efforts to encourage
their growth. His sense of humor makes our office an
enjoyable place to work. Arv leads us while, at the same,
motivates us so that we are inspired with confidence and
self-reliance and provided with additional insight and
energy to accomplish our tasks.

These letters offer good examples of bosses who understand that patience and self-discipline create an atmosphere in the workplace that is appreciated by their employees. The compliments and comments by their employees verify this. They describe bosses as "cool," "pleasant," "good-humored," "considerate," "soft-spoken," and so on. Yet these businesses are not isolated on some peaceful, tranquil island in the South Seas. These employees describe work situations that are not pictured as the most serene imaginable. Think for a minute. There is nothing more stressful than dealing with people who are at the "end of their financial road" and forced to declare bankruptcy or who must organize and keep decorum at a county hospital where there is a crisis a minute with patients and staff. But if an attorney handling a caseload of over three thousand bankruptcies can stay calm and thoughtful to his staff in the midst of stressful encounters, and if a county hospital administrator never "loses her cool" and brings out the best in her staff, then there is hope for every boss, regardless of the situation or working environment. Whatever methods these bosses have discovered definitely work, and I'll be willing to bet that they practice this same self-discipline throughout every phase of their lives—not just between the hours of nine and five. And when they do, everyone on their team feels respected and special.

Practiced TEAMWORK Makes Perfect

When I think about the various factors that go into creating an atmosphere of understanding and practicing tolerance in the workplace, I am reminded of an acronym that I share with my audiences and employees. In the final analysis, how we treat the people we work with, and particularly how bosses treat employees, creates either an enjoyable working environment or a place of dread. Consider for a moment the different thoughts in the acronym that all mean the same thing. They all seem to boil down to a matter of respecting others. When you show respect for others, everything else comes into perspective.

TEAMWORK

TOGETHER................Working together rather than as an individual, you can make things happen more easily and professionally.

EMPATHY....................For fellow employees; concern about their well-being.

ASSIST........................The ability and desire to help others when they need assistance.

MATURITY.................Be mature in handling problems and challenges in a positive, constructive manner.

WILLINGNESS..........To work with people throughout the company in a friendly, cooperative manner.

ORGANIZATION......Be professionally organized to reduce crisis situations with the help of other employees and departments.

RESPECT.....................For people you work with on a daily basis.

KINDNESS.................For all people you come in contact with.

It is important that all eight letters are implemented on a daily basis if bosses and employees are to have a true feeling of what TEAMWORK is all about!

Displaying empathy, maturity, respect, and kindness doesn't just happen. You can't put a group of words on a blackboard and expect everyone instantly to get with the program. By controlling our mouths, looks, and actions, however, we can make the first step toward being actively involved with the true meaning of *teamwork*. All of the managers at our companies are informed that the employees don't work *for* bosses, but *with* bosses. This is the true meaning of "teamwork."

You won't find "teamwork" a part of the vocabulary of the next two bosses. Their antics have terrorized their teams to the point that employees felt the need to expose them publicly. Surprisingly, however, both employees still worked for these individuals when they wrote their letters and entered our contest.

A Psycho at Work

THIS IS A TRUE STORY and "psycho" is a mild word to describe my boss. Employees would brief each other about his mood upon his arrival by asking, "How's the weather?" His moods would vary from one

minute to the next, but you could be assured they would
be mostly bad.

Employees were always prepared to duck because the
dirty looks and flying objects might hit you or kill you. We
never knew the cause of his anger. It might be some
obscure reason that caused the rages, broken coffeepots,
mirrors, and smashed computer keyboards. It was like a
demolition derby when it came to watching his tirades with
smashing phones and a state-of-the-art fax machine.

One day I had a garment on a dress form. He didn't like
it. So the boss whipped out his knife and slashed the garment and dress form to shreds. We moved into a building
that had decorator-padded walls. This really suited our resi-
dent psycho, because when he was in one of his moods, he
got out his knife and slashed the wall!

Raging Chief

OF ALL PEOPLE, you would expect a police chief to
be self-controlled. This isn't the case with my chief. He
has a very, very bad temper. He explodes at officers and
screams obscenities at the drop of a hat.

Once an article was printed that was critical of the operation of our department. The chief slammed his door so
hard that the carpenters had to replace the door frame. In
a discussion with one of the officers, the chief took off his
badge and threw it at the officer, saying, "If you think you
can run the place better, you can be chief."

On many occasions when the chief is angry, he throws a
phone down the hallway in the direction of an officer, and
knocks over bookshelves that are full of books. On yet
another occasion, the chief became enraged in the briefing
room as an officer cracked a joke. He leaped into the officer's face, swearing at him. Later, the chief called the officer
into his office to apologize and when the officer continued to
act a little miffed, the chief started screaming all over again.

When he learned some of the officers had a meeting with
the school board and he hadn't been informed, he was furi-
ous. He retaliated by bringing in a whole plate of jalapeno
peppers, announcing that they were "donuts" for the officers!

All I can say is that if I worked for either of these bosses, I would be looking for another place of employment.

"If only..."

Rudyard Kipling said it so well in his poem "If." In stanza after stanza, he instructs us about the importance of self-control and self-discipline. He writes about the acts that make us not just grow up, but grow up well. To share some of his thoughts briefly:

> *If you keep your head when all about you*
> *Are losing theirs and blaming it on you...*
> *If you can wait and not be tired by waiting,*
> *Or, being lied about, don't deal in lies,*
> *Or, being hated, don't give way to hating,*
> *And yet don't look too good, nor walk too wise...*
> *If you can bear to hear the truth you've spoken*
> *Twisted by knaves to make a trap for fools...*
> *If you can fill the unforgiving minute*
> *With sixty seconds' worth of distance run—*
> *Yours is the Earth and everything that's in it,*
> *And—which is more—you'll be a Man, my son!*

Yes, we've all heard it before—*IF*—but Kipling's advice is as sound today as it was one hundred years ago.

Below are excerpts from letters about some good bosses with the right idea. Let's see what methods they use to show an even-tempered, disciplined attitude that employees appreciate.

A Cool Dude at Work and at Home

OUR COMPANY was on the verge of collapsing and the employees were under great stress, not knowing what was going to happen to their jobs. Wally's steadfast professionalism has helped us through it all. His approach to managing our group of programmer/analysts is organized, efficient, and humble.

Wally is always polite and respectful, even to those who give him trouble. When things go wrong, Wally doesn't start chewing people out; his mind immediately jumps to suggestions for solutions. Even when overstressed, he NEVER raises his voice in anger or agitation. When others are over-stressed, he asks how he can help, or he tries to rethink our priorities so that we can just concentrate on the next task.

He never resorts to crude or obscene language, or to sarcasm. He isn't a stuffed shirt; he likes a joke, even when it's on himself. When praised or recognized for his accomplishments, he can't hide his embarrassment.

I think Wally's strength as an effective leader comes from genuine respect for his employees, and *patience, patience, patience.* To top it all off, his wife says he acts the same way at home—with their *teenager!* No, he's not perfect, but he is certainly my best boss ever and he could definitely give other bosses lessons!

A Low-Key Manager Who Gets Results

IN THE TEN YEARS I've worked for Wayne, I have never heard him raise his voice, berate, or publicly criticize one of his employees. Project problems and criticisms are discussed in private, face-to-face. He maintains an open-door office policy at all times. His easy demeanor, fair treatment of employees, and low-key approach to problem solving make the office atmosphere friendly and easy to work within.

He is such a personable man, good-natured with a good sense of humor. The quality is infectious, resulting in his employees' responding in kind. He trusts us to work hard, meet our deadlines, and excel at our jobs. Chances for promotions, different jobs, or additional training are made available to the whole office. Three of his past employees have been promoted to management positions with his help and encouragement. Employees who have left for other jobs routinely stay in touch with him by letter and visit frequently.

On a personal level Wayne takes an interest in the family of each employee. His interest has included baby-sitting for many of us, as well as social dinners and a yearly fish fry. He makes it clear that we should not take our jobs home with us at night to interfere with our family life.

Wayne works at improving his management skills constantly while never losing sight of his employees and their needs. His easy demeanor, trust of employees, support, and sense of humor make him the best boss I've ever had.

Now, these are great bosses, of course. Anyone would like to work for one of them. You have to admire someone who *never* raises his voice in anger, even to a *teenager*. This man truly does have the patience of Job! As a way of summarizing this section, let's be realistic and admit that almost all of us lose our cool every once in a while. Therefore, we could all work on being more understanding and patient with those around us. It is part of our character that can always be improved, and the rewards for doing so are incredible.

The Corporate Coach's Comments

There are some people who seem to have a knack for knowing how to "get to" others. They know which "buttons to push," and continually seem to take great delight in doing so. Most of us have had teenagers under our roof at one time or another. They seem to be masters of the art of pulling the chains of parents, teachers, or even their own friends. But some employees also have refined button-pushing into an art form. In fact, it is entirely possible that the boss you consider quick-tempered is merely responding to having his buttons pushed by one or more employees. This doesn't make his tantrums any easier to tolerate, but it does give us hope for controlling the outbursts by redirecting the button-pushers.

Some of us unknowingly do things that annoy our bosses. It doesn't take a rocket scientist to figure out which things we say or do that send the boss into "slow burn," which often results in a temper outburst.

Let's apply a little common sense here. If we know that the red cape irritates the bull, don't wave it in front of him. If we know what annoys and provokes an outburst from the boss—*don't do it!* It's as simple as that.

This still leaves us with the boss whose employees historically dance around on eggshells, because he's a walking time bomb. I can only suggest a very cautious, indulgent approach to this boss. If you don't know what triggers his rage, it's hard to know how to avoid it. I would suggest, though, that the first rule when approaching any boss with a problem, especially one who has a volatile temper, is to pick the most opportune moment. Make sure he's happy, ideally just after a big sale, before you attempt to approach him about how his blowups affect the climate of the office. You should appeal to his "good nature" at this happy moment to share with him your concern about the tension at work. He honestly may not be aware of this. Some bosses vent just to feel important without giving much thought to how it affects the workforce. Even if the boss is angry after this discussion, at least he's been reminded that his behavior is causing a problem. Possibly, he'll even try to fix it!

Confide in your boss that you certainly understand how the pressures of business are very stressful, particularly for managers. Tell him you have a feeling that, if he would gather his people around him as team players with him as the coach and create a friendly atmosphere in which to work, he would find his company becoming even more successful. Be positive. Do not accuse, blame, or point fingers. Spread the fault among everyone, and tell him that you're ready to do your part.

You are taking a risk any time you venture into the constructive criticism arena with an ill-tempered boss, but there is also a possibility the fellow just might react favorably to your helping hand. If this strategy doesn't work and you've managed to set off another forest fire, just run for the door before you get burned again.

Coach's Corner

TO THE EMPLOYEE:

☛ Think about ways you might be inadvertently "pushing the boss's buttons" to provoke a temper tantrum.

☛ Make a conscious effort to think before you say anything or do anything that might bring out your boss's temper and violence.

☛ Don't play games. Be direct, honest, and never manipulate your boss.

☛ Try to understand some of the pressures that may be causing the boss to be stressed out.

☛ Remember that a boss's words said in anger may not truly reflect his feelings–sometimes you've got to cut the boss a little slack.

☛ Decide whether working for a boss who "goes through the roof" despite all your efforts to calm him is worth all the effort, and if not, look for a boss who respects employees by remaining cool in the face of tension and stress.

TO THE BOSS:

☛ Consider events or people in your company that provoke your anger and attempt to "nip the irritation in the bud."

☛ Address problem-causing issues *before* they cause your irritation.

☛ Practice some self-control in times of stress by taking a deep breath, counting to ten, thinking of the consequences of your words and actions, smiling at the person or problem, and proceeding carefully.

☛ Treat employees with respect and dignity, trying to see both sides of issues, and you will notice the increase in employee morale.

☞ Provide employees a professional role model that projects maturity, kindness, and teamwork. You will be amazed at how quickly employees pattern themselves after someone they respect and admire.

☞ Remember that words said in anger cannot be retrieved.

☞ Weed out any employee who has a negative effect on the success of your company with their game-playing or manipulation.

Director's Office

CHAPTER 12

Office Politicians and Square Dealers

WE'VE HEARD THE TERM "political animal" for years and associate it mostly with someone seeking elected public office. In reality, we see more political maneuvering in the workplace than ever existed in the seats of government around the world. It's painfully obvious in the management of some companies, but it's just as prevalent in the workforce. Look around you. Not a day passes that you aren't exposed to someone's politicking, whether it's a telephone solicitation, a coworker desiring your help on a project, or even a teenager wanting to borrow the family car. I call it "schmoozing," but the meaning is similar and the possibilities are endless.

Whether we pass these attempts off as sales efforts, trade-offs, free enterprise, entrepreneurship, marketing expertise, or pure flattery, they are nonetheless forms of a politician in action. They are a part of everyday life. They have become a way of doing business.

The real problem surfaces when schmoozing turns into a spoils system of favoritism in the workplace. Where some employees are given preferential treatment over others, you will find a morale problem. Where bosses use political intrigue for personal advancement, for manipulation, or for mere amusement, you will find a morale problem. And where you find an employee morale problem, you will find a company in trouble.

The bosses below have gone way beyond schmoozing. They have become political machines themselves as they maneuver and manipulate employees for their own self-interests. Some even go so far as to risk litigation for their discriminatory practices.

SINCE I WAS TRANSFERRED to my current boss, my creative spirit has been destroyed; as has been my self-esteem, morale, confidence, and health. She enjoys causing people grief. She constantly tells other division directors and employees about several *horrible* members of her staff. She makes certain the supervisors, who try to work with their employees and attempt to keep morale high, are not given pay raises. There are those who are "her people" and she covers up or downplays their mistakes, and overreacts to mistakes of staff members whom she hates. She sets you up, if she doesn't like you, by giving you a specific order or directive and then reprimands you for doing what she initially told you to do by twisting events and evidence. She even suggests that staff can gain promotions by snitching on their fellow employees.

∾

MY BOSS IS THE COLDEST, most vicious woman I've ever met, and she runs her business like a concentration camp! She takes aside one person at a time and poisons his mind against the other people in the office, saying people don't like that person. She fights with her husband, who co-owns the company with her, in front of everyone. Not a day passes that we don't hear profanities flying and doors slamming throughout the offices. Employees dread her entrance into their offices; it can only mean trouble is a-brew!

∾

MY BOSS ROUTINELY has found ways to cheat me out of my commissions, although my sales have contributed to increase our company's sales volume from fifty thousand dollars annually to well over a million dollars. Now she's found a boyfriend—a retail clerk in a hardware store. She hired him, doubled his salary, made him chief of operations, and took one hundred dollars a month away from my medical benefits to create top coverage for him. He now has his eye on my sales and marketing position, and it's only a matter of time!

~

MY BOSS IS NOTORIOUS for her favoritism. She takes her
"favorites" for extended lunches with her at least twice a
week. If anyone else in the office is late returning from
lunch, she leaves a nasty note on their desk. She overlooks
behavior of one of her "favorites" that was contrary to our
company policy, but tried to have someone else fired for
doing the same thing. She usually doesn't work a forty-
hour week by leaving early and coming in late. She excuses
this by saying, "Supervisors are different."

~

WITH NO MANAGERIAL SKILLS, she goes about browbeating most employees on a daily basis. There is no reward for
working harder because she won't deliver on promised raises, although she finds the money for her "friends." Her
friends get raises and promotions—in spite of corporate
money problems—even though they haven't earned them
through work, nor are they the best candidates for the new
position. She uses her position to protect her friends from
creditors and from the corporate officials when the friend's
mismanagement led to her losing $30,000 worth of invento-
ry. The friend wasn't reprimanded nor did she lose her job.

~

HE'S A REAL LADIES' man and, of course, he's ready to
make any woman's job easier for some favors in the office.
In fact, he has been seen coming out of his office with his
secretary, straightening his pants while she's pulling down
her skirt. He lets her boss people around and make departmental decisions. It doesn't matter how many years you
have on the job, if he likes someone—even if they have only
been here six months—he'll put them in for a promotion.

~

WE'VE BEEN WITHOUT raises for three years, except for
the boss's son who was getting his allowance via the payroll so he could take the pay stub to the work experience

teacher to show his employment, thus earning high school credits. His "salary" increased 325 percent in one year! He hasn't even seen the inside of the office and on paydays, his mother delivers his paycheck to him at home!

These bosses have been identified by employees as ultimate practicers of "cronyism," although they have yet to be held responsible for their actions. The numerous references to and complaints about nepotism are all too common in companies across this country. We see it not only in family-owned businesses, but also in the Fortune 500. It ranges from granting family members summer intern jobs when permanent employees are laid off or cut back on hours, to blatant firing of a competent, tenured worker in order to replace him with a family member. I've actually heard a company president admit, "There's nothing wrong with nepotism, as long as you keep it in the family!"

As we see, people view their position as "boss" differently. Some see it as carte blanche to do anything and everything that suits them without regard for those about them. Others see it as a reward for their achievements and an opportunity for future growth for themselves and those they manage.

Spoils of the Office

It might appear that those of us who have reached a responsible position in management should be able to sit back and rest on our laurels without a lot of thought given to the continuous upward climb on the ladder of success. It might seem that, after struggling for years through the maze in corporate America, success would become its own reward. After all, maybe we should be enjoying the *spoils of office*. Right? I know some managers who interpret this to mean that they have earned the luxury of delegating responsibility. And that's okay. If, after a successful business career a person wants to sit back and take it easy, that's fine so long as he remembers that the others who work for him don't have the same luxury. They still need to earn a living and build a career, and for them, the boss's desire to "take it easy" is irrelevant. These bosses need to make sure that if they're going out to pasture they leave the business in the hands of someone who will tend the store and continue to provide a quality work environment for the employees. If that's not possible, the boss should officially retire or sell the business and get out of the way so that those who are left can earn a living.

Now, "the spoils" take on different meanings to different bosses. Some look at it as an opportunity to share profits in the company with all employees in the form of 401K programs and retirement plans. Others see it as a means to "feather their own nest" with amenities so luxurious as to embarrass visiting aristocracy, while employees toil in unfit surroundings. Wouldn't it be terrific if bosses could visualize how dealing squarely with employees instead of playing favorites can help the company and the boss?

It's easy to understand that a boss, who looks for opportunities to share equitably the "spoils of office" with all employees, will earn respect and credibility with his employees. And we aren't talking about just money here.

A successful manager truly views distributing the *spoils of office* as an opportunity to share the wealth of his experience and knowledge and to assume the position of mentor and *coach*. This boss usually makes his first task a determined effort to see that everyone in the company gets to "play on a level field"—where employees are judged on the basis of their qualifications and achievements, rather than a preferential "buddy system."

You've read the letters in this chapter, which described situation after situation in which employees were discriminated against, treated unfairly, and became victims of a political machine running full speed downhill at a company. It's inevitable that you can't continually play with people's minds and lives and expect them to be loyal, happy employees. The following bosses certainly have discovered this. Let's see how they deal squarely and equitably with all their employees.

*PRIOR TO OUR BOSS'S ARRIVAL, our semiannual production reviews were looked upon with dread. Management seemed to dwell on any negatives, and gloss over positives. He changed the review policy to allow all employees to write their own reviews. Employees could emphasize their contributions, as well as suggest areas for improvement. It was the molding of our unit into the company's highest achieving and happiest team that was his crowning achievement. A great part of that transformation grew from his use of *the huddle*. Huddles are used by sports teams to foster team spirit and camaraderie, but I'd never seen them used by business "teams." It sounded corny at first, but we hunch together in a circle, and throw our arms around each others' shoulders. The result was an increase in morale and team unity that was undeniable.

∽

I BEGAN WORKING for my boss and his wife over twenty-five years ago. Over the years I have now worked for three generations of their family. My boss told me early on that I worked *with* him, not *for* him. He said that I should treat their family-owned rental office as if it were my own. It's been the same with each generation and I have been treated just like a member of the family. We have shared sorrow and pain, as well as joy and happiness, over our children, our parents, and experiences that life has dealt us.

∽

FOR YEARS our "bosses" had intimidated us by referring to us as *warm bodies*. When Bob came on board, he brought a new philosophy. He felt training can produce a good coach, but great coaches are born and raised with good values and high morals. He was a shining example of compassion, character, and principles. He made each employee feel appreciated and special. He initiated team meetings at our plant and never felt intimidated by the power of a team. He kept each employee motivated with praise, encouraged independence, and implemented our suggestions. His attitude vitalized our team. He had the wisdom to know that the company would benefit when the employees are motivated to do their best for their own personal satisfaction.

∽

DESPITE HAVING LOST A LEG in the war, Stan began his twelve-hour days at 5:00 A.M. to create time to mentor to

each of his employees. Day after day, his "Good morning"
greeting was followed by a suggestion that we read an
interesting engineering journal article. One day he suggested
that three of us enroll in graduate school and dismissed our
concerns about not being qualified, assuring us that we
were. He convinced his superiors to invent flexible work
schedules so each of us could attend class and to provide
some financial support. For years I wondered how Stan
had convinced management to support us. Shortly after he
retired, I discovered a photocopy of a handwritten letter he
had given to his boss: "You and I are the past of this organization. Our job now is to ensure the future. We can do so
by grooming our best and brightest to be leaders. You wonder if we can afford the cost of doing so. I assure you we
cannot afford the costs of *not* doing so."

∽

OUR BOSS IS FAIR, honest, and not all-consumed in his
powerful position as the head of a state federal law enforce-
ment agency. He trusts each of his employees and respects
us as individuals. He laughs heartily and is one of us, yet we
always know who is the captain of the ship. Ron restored
dignity to a group who was cursed with a monster boss for
years and had been browbeaten to the point of losing hope.

∽

WE ARE SO FORTUNATE to have an entire management
team who believes in the unique qualities of each staff
member. Our team is special because there are no "power
struggles" and no one possesses a "knowledge is power"
attitude. Employees don't compete against each other, only
against ourselves. There is seldom a day I don't look forward to coming to work. If I were forced to single out only
one manager as my choice, it would Marsha because she is
always so appreciative of the work we do. She has just
been assigned to another position, but she left me with this
thought; "Now you have the stars you are always reaching
for. I have enjoyed being with you for part of your ride."

There's little question how employees regard their bosses who deal honestly and squarely with them on an impartial basis. Several phrases come immediately to mind: "I'm treated like a member of the family," "he's consistent with all employees," "he encouraged and praised all of us." I've said it before in this book, but it bears repeating. *When employees feel they are treated well, they are willing to "go that extra mile" for the company and for the boss!*

The Extra Mile

Quality and equitable treatment of employees establishes a climate from nine to five that seems to make the clock disappear. When people are treated fairly and aboveboard, they feel appreciated and special—they are not just names on the company employee roster. They enjoy coming to work because they feel like part of a family, part of a team. They want to contribute and feel their contribution makes a difference for the company. They put more of themselves into their jobs. They don't seem to mind short deadlines as much. They are willing to share responsibilities with coworkers. They are more willing to spend whatever time is necessary to help a customer. In short, they are willing to "go the extra mile" to get the job done.

That's a win-win situation for the employee, for the company, and for the boss. But let me mention one additional ingredient that will encourage an employee to go the extra mile for the boss and the company. It's being recognized for his contribution to the team not only by the boss, but by his teammates. Peer approval is important to us all. This is particularly true of those we work with on a daily basis. Let me share my own experience regarding this point.

Each of our companies uses an attractive, personalized certificate for employees to show their appreciation to their coworkers. *You've Been Caught Doing Something Good!* or *You are TERRIFIC!* certificates can be seen displayed throughout our buildings. They are found on employees' workstations, on their computer terminals, or in their trucks. When someone—anyone in our company— catches someone else doing something exceptional, that person can issue one of these certificates. Not only does the employee's name appear on the certificate, but also listed is the reason for the recognition. In addition, the certificate is signed by the manager or supervisor, who must authorize the certificate. So you can see, the certificates aren't "a dime a dozen" but rather very special indeed to the giver and the receiver.

Employees are much more willing to "go that extra mile" for a boss who respects and appreciates his employees. As we know, an extra "inch," much less an extra mile, is an effort for an employee who is on the outside looking into a political ring where the boss elected himself king. The next two letters about office politicians prove my point.

A Politician Who Didn't Run for Office

HE'S THE BIGGEST PLAYER in the political ring outside of Washington! If he likes you, you'll get to go on training classes, your promotion is guaranteed, employee-of-the-month cash award is granted, your annual evaluation is outstanding, and a yearly bonus is delivered. He treats you like a best, trusted friend.

If you're not his pet, he will harass and intimidate you by belittling your work performance and professional qualification. Any questions you direct to him will be responded to with a sarcastic remark to prevent you from asking further.

He disallows creativity, provides neither guidance nor information, yet he expects you to do an excellent job on a project. His behavior inspires an unpleasant atmosphere and unfriendly attitude among the employees. It damages our morale and work quality. It drives away people who are highly qualified and enthusiastic about their work, like me, because I feel there is no reward for a job well done. There is no incentive for me to do a good job.

Good Ol' Boy at Work

HE'S A LOUD, OBNOXIOUS, OUTGOING ex-salesman who bought a business and came into the company, thinking that he would be a "good ol' boy" to the staff. He quickly developed favorites at his small company of twelve employees, and hands out bonuses, raises, and extra days off to them at will. Favorites are picked by how an employee strokes the boss and how attractive the employee is—never on how well they do their job.

Management hears from the boss that he is behind them 100 percent, but I can't remember one rule or decision that wasn't undermined by the boss. For example, our lunch hours have to be taken between 11:30 A.M. and 2:30 P.M. Privately, he tells one of his favorites that he can take lunch at the end of the day if he would like to do so.

He only wants to hear good things about the business and himself, so he discontinued our office management meetings two years ago. With no direction or support, our managers do their best knowing that the boss will start his rumor mill about them if they bring him any bad news.

His rumor mill is when he goes to one employee to talk about another, then turns the table and talks to the other employee about the first employee. This creates a lot of bad feelings based on false rumors. He wants to be the only "good guy" so he makes sure everyone else is at odds with each other. He also is quick to point out that anyone not in sales or service is "nothing but overhead."

It certainly doesn't sound as if either of the above politicians could "buy" the votes of their employees. I can assure you it will come back to haunt them later on.

As we all know, credibility and respect are earned by the way we treat others. This is especially true in our bosses. We may respect the title, but not necessarily the person wearing it. The two bosses described below have earned not only credibility and respect from their employees, they have earned loyalty.

∾

A Father-Daughter Tag Team

OUR FAMILY-OWNED COMPANY brings joy to everyone who eats our product: ice cream cones. Our father and daughter team hasn't let success go to their heads as they always ask for our input, form employee committees to make our plant more efficient, find time for new employees, and visit the hospital whenever an employee is injured.

They also make sure that we have a ride to work if we have transportation problems. With so many depending on this company for our livelihood, our bosses take the initiative to find us another job when occasional seasonal layoffs are necessary. We always know, however, we will be recalled at their first opportunity. They show exceptional leadership and great business sense, along with compassion, understanding, and thoughtfulness for their employees. We have all the usual company benefits, in addition to no-interest loans at any time there is a need, paid employee meetings with lunch, attendance points for free gifts, safety lotteries, gifts for newlyweds and babies, summer and Christmas bonus programs, Christmas gifts, and parties throughout the year.

Director of "Equality"

I'VE BEEN FORTUNATE to work for Mark for seven years. During that time he has consistently dealt with his employees in the same evenhanded, straightforward manner. In his dual position of director of MIS and Electronic Service Operations, he coordinates activities between all departments and he is considerate of everyone's feelings.

When a problem arises, employees know that while they may approach Mark and explain the problem, he expects them also to have a solution or suggestion to solve the problem. He constantly builds all the employees' pride in their own skills since he does use their suggestions when appropriate. He gives praise publicly to every team member when warranted, but any inner-office turmoil is addressed behind closed doors. He approaches any situation with one eye on corporate policy and the other on solving the problem in the most equitable manner possible.

Mark will listen to all his employees' personal problems without becoming overly involved, while allowing flexible schedules to give them the opportunity to address their problems without the additional stress of an angry boss.

He brings doughnuts every Friday for everyone to enjoy and throws get-togethers at his house for the entire department.

The first letter brought a sense of déjà vu because many of the philosophies and concepts were the same ones that we implemented when we started our business almost three decades ago in Texas. The principles of a successful family-owned and operated business differ only slightly from those of large corporations. The five steps that I stress in my seminars on "How to Thrive and Survive in a Family Business" are:

Challenge
Communication
Respect
Compensation
Love

Whether you are dealing with a family member, a colleague, an employee, or a customer, these components form the synergy of teamwork. There's no question that the two bosses above have captured this vision.

The Corporate Coach's Comments

How many times have we interviewed for a new job, been excited with the prospects for that company's future, found the job description matched our background and experience perfectly, and been hired by a boss who seemed too good to be true? The first week on the job can certainly be an eye-opener. Right? Some of us are lucky and the company, the job, and the boss are exactly as perceived in our initial interview. Others of us walk into the old "buddy system" where the chosen few reign like monarchy and the rest of the employees work, unappreciated, like slave labor. And for employees in the latter group the hours between nine and five can seem endless.

What can someone on the "outside" do to be accepted by the crowd? The obvious answer would be that the talent for which we were hired should do the trick, especially if hard work and dedicated effort are coupled with that talent.

Unfortunately, in politically oriented offices, this doesn't always ring true.

If you're faced with a hard-nosed political boss who doesn't warm to a hardworking, efficient employee with a pleasant personality, you need to do some planning of your own. If you are dealing with a boss who disregards specific company policies for certain employees, make sure you have a copy of the Employee Handbook. If your company has had constant employee turnover because others haven't been able to outlast the boss's cronyism, make sure you have the most recent turnover figures documented. If safety procedures are being ignored by the boss's buddies, make sure you have a copy of the OSHA guidebook. If you are dealing with specific discrimination issues that could create legal repercussions for the company, list them on a piece of paper. In other words, if you have specific areas where favoritism is harming the company and its image, make sure you have them documented. You also might think about individual grievances and write down specific events that you consider to be particularly problematic.

Now ask to have a meeting with the boss at his convenience. Remember, whenever we are dealing with a boss who doesn't respect his employees and treats them in such a manner as to have caused a particular problem, timing is everything. Pick a moment when he is in a good mood!

Explain to the boss that the employees appreciate the company and their jobs and the entire group wants to do the best job possible at all times. Cite a couple of instances in each area of concern: company policy violations; safety infractions; employee turnover facts and figures; possible legal problems, etc. You also might confide that he's dealing with people and as such, he's dealing with feelings and sensitivities at times. Delicately point out some areas where his acts of favoritism have crushed employees' spirit and self-esteem. Ask him if he was aware of this and would be willing to reexamine areas where violations are endangering the company. Ask him if he would be willing to use a little more consideration toward the feelings of all the employees so that everyone can feel they are a valued member of the team.

Most bosses realize that an overall team effort will add much more growth and bottom-line profit to a company than the contributions of just a few friends. Even office politicians are more concerned with the bottom line than they are about their special-interest groups.

Coach's Corner

TO THE EMPLOYEE:

☛ Make sure that your job performance and attitude are above reproach and don't provide any justification for your boss's tendency to treat you unjustly.

☛ Deal openly and aboveboard at all times with everyone in the company, which should be an inspiration to anyone who leans toward office politics.

☛ Treat all employees and the boss with respect and don't take sides with warring factions so as not to add fuel to any prejudicial fire.

☛ Avoid office politics yourself. Keep your record clean.

☛ Cast your vote for another boss and company if all reasonable efforts fail to persuade your office politician to treat all employees equally.

TO THE BOSS:

☛ Consider every employee equally as an asset and don't show preferential treatment to anyone. Employees like to know the rules and the privileges apply to everyone equally.

☛ Think about the positive effect of a team all working together for the best of the company. It stands to reason that a team outperforms a group of individuals every time.

☛ Provide your employees a professional role model by not taking sides on issues merely based on friendship or family relationship.

☛ Encourage an atmosphere of teamwork in your company.

☛ Think honestly about what would happen if all of those who aren't your cronies decided to let you and your buddies run the company without their help.

CHAPTER 13

Conclusion

I TOYED WITH THE IDEA of concluding this book with a "best of the best and worst of the worst" chapter. But I think you'll agree that it would be nearly impossible to pick a best and a worst from the examples that you've read. I know that some of them seem so outlandish that you may doubt their authenticity, but let me assure you that I have not fabricated any of them. They are all legitimate entries to one of our annual contests. In fact, there are any number of equally unbelievable stories that could have been included.

As I've mentioned earlier, the ratio of contest entries is about seven bad bosses for one good boss. Aside from the normal tendency of people to be more likely to take the time to write about a bad situation than about a good one, this tells me that there are too many bad bosses. While there might actually be more good bosses than bad ones, it is obvious that too many people have not thought about what it means to be a boss. Wherever these people go, they leave a trail of anguish, anger, frustration, low productivity, absenteeism, and high rates of wasteful employee turnover. The cumulative effect of their dishonesty, incompetence, or lack of consideration is a national tragedy which comes with a considerable dollars-and-cents price tag, above and beyond the wear and tear on our mental and physical health.

For this reason, I am hoping that we can start a revolution in our workplaces. We should be able to get the same sort of respect and courtesy at work that we expect at home. After all, we spend as much or more time on the job as we do at home. Imagine how much more productive we'd be, how many fewer sick days there'd be, how much less time we'd have to spend training new workers, and how much happier we'd be—all this for a simple no-cost change in the way we relate with each other.

The revolution can start right here. This book is a mirror of our national workplace. It can be your mirror, too. Did you see yourself somewhere in it? If so, I hope that it was in one of the letters about good bosses, but if not, then do something about it. Being a good boss is not all that hard. Aside from technical competence, it requires only that you think of the people with whom you work as people, not as work units; that you deal with them honestly and fairly; that you are courteous and considerate—in other words, that you treat them the way you'd like to be treated. If you think that any of the traits we've identified in bad bosses—being authoritarian, being insensitive to the feelings of those working for you, etc.—are necessary to get the job done, then you're sadly mistaken. Always remember—the secret to success in the business world is happy employees and happy customers. And it's hard to have happy customers without happy employees.

To Contact Jim Miller

Jim Miller can be reached for keynote speeches, seminars, and motivational presentations through:

JIM MILLER ENTERPRISES, INC.
2261 Brookhollow Plaza Drive, Suite 301
Arlington, Texas 76006
(817) 640-2403

Popular current presentation titles include:

ROAD MAP FOR SUCCESS
- How to Feel Like a Million Without Spending a Nickel!
- Corporate Coaching
- How to Profit Through Service and Teamwork
- Providing Sales Leadership for Your Growth
- How to Thrive and Survive in a Family Business

In addition to the above topics, new programs constantly are being introduced in order to respond to changes in workplace conditions and industry needs. Jim Miller customizes his presentations to each client's needs.

There are few speakers who have the enthusiasm and electric spark to motivate a group as Jim Miller does. He keeps his audiences both entertained and totally involved, and he always leaves them with positive formulas that they can successfully use on a daily basis in both their business and their personal lives. Participants in Jim's seminars often have said, "Hearing Jim Miller was like getting a transfusion of new blood."